PRAISE FOR *DESTINED TO WIN*

Destined to Win is a practical tool that will help you discover your purpose and destiny. In each chapter, Kris explains simple keys to live your life as a champion, and how to rise to the call of God on your life. If you want to learn how to be victorious in your life, you won't want to miss this book. Kris has keen insight into how God's people encounter God's power and then give expression to it in their life and walk in it together in community. He is a shepherd after God's heart and speaks from his experience of God's heart.

—MIKE BICKLE, INTERNATIONAL HOUSE OF PRAYER OF KANSAS CITY

Deep inside every believer's heart is a dream. For some it may be buried beneath the fear of failure, hidden by insecurity, clouded by self-doubt, or hindered by not knowing who they are in Christ, but the dream is there. Each of us has a God-given desire to play our part in changing the world. However, you cannot simply uncover the dreams in your heart. You must also move toward them. Too easily we get stuck about what to do next. But God sends people into our lives who walk with us and encourage us to pursue our dreams. For twenty years, Kris Vallotton has been one of those people for me. In my early 20s I would tell Kris, with great excitement, about the things God placed on my heart. They were massive dreams and I had no idea how I would ever get there. Kris not only believed in my dreams, but helped shape me as I moved toward the call of God on my life. *Destined to Win* will both encourage and challenge you with insight and the necessary tools to not only uncover your dreams, but also set you on the course of seeing your dreams become reality.

—BANNING LIEBSCHER, FOUNDER AND PASTOR OF JESUS CULTURE AND
AUTHOR OF *ROOTED: THE HIDDEN PLACES WHERE GOD DEVELOPS YOU*

Destined to Win is encouraging, inspiring, and challenging us to embrace and step toward our dreams. Kris Vallotton is one of the best I know in showing the heart of God as a Dream Champion ready to lead us all into victory. He does it again with *Destined to Win*. I invite you into a journey to see how the best of you can be both "hidden in Christ" and drawn to the surface to glorify our Father. As I read these pages I am reminded that there is still much left in my life to bring forth for the One who gave everything for me. I highly recommend you get this book and apply it to your destiny!

—DANNY SILK, AUTHOR OF *CULTURE OF HONOR*, *LOVING OUR KIDS ON PURPOSE*, *POWERFUL AND FREE*, AND *KEEP YOUR LOVE ON*

Hardships try to hold us back and tear us down. But in *Destined to Win*, my friend Kris shows us how to relentlessly rise above life's storms. The wisdom in this book has unmatched potential to encourage and guide you on your journey to success.

—JOHN BEVERE, AUTHOR/MINISTER OF MESSENGER INTERNATIONAL

All of life is a story and Kris Vallotton is a master storyteller. In *Destined to Win*, he connects with our hearts and beautifully guides us on a journey of discovering our identity in an often confusing world. A must read if you long to find healing and power in this life, not only the life beyond. Bravo!

—TED DEKKER, *NEW YORK TIMES* BESTSELLING AUTHOR OF MORE THAN 30 BOOKS

Kris Vallotton's faith is contagious. That's the point. Read this book and catch it—and then try not to spread it around yourself. You'll fail miserably. Have fun!

—ERIC METAXAS, #1 *NEW YORK TIMES* BESTSELLING AUTHOR, NATIONALLY SYNDICATED RADIO HOST

Destined to Win is filled with practical steps to help you realize the fullness of who you were created to be. Using examples from his own life, Kris shows us that we all can achieve greatness, first by defeating our internal enemies, then by following a few simple, but profoundly wise, principles, such as believing you were created for a purpose, allowing God to turn your weakness into strength, and surrounding yourself with different perspectives and gifts. I love how Kris puts greatness within the reach of every person.

—STACEY CAMPBELL, FOUNDER OF NEW LIFE CHURCH AND BE A HERO

Destined to Win is good fruit from the deep passion and gifting my dear friend Kris Vallotton has to equip people to actualize their divine purposes. As usual for Kris' powerful library of written work, *Destined to Win* is insightful, practical, incredibly personal, biblically sound, and profoundly hopeful—reminding us that our desire for significance is not only okay, but that it is God-given. In fact, Kris does an excellent job of giving each reader license to be their authentic selves—set free of performance, hiding, and fear of failure through the overwhelming love of God—and releases them to encounter the anointing of God that was always meant to impact the Kingdom through the *real* them. *Destined to Win* even reveals the purpose behind our pain and offers encouragement for the struggle of walking in our destiny and trusting our good Father, who has set us up for Kingdom success.

—DR. CHÉ AHN, PRESIDENT OF HARVEST INTERNATIONAL MINISTRY,
FOUNDING PASTOR OF HROCK CHURCH IN PASADENA, CA, AND
INTERNATIONAL CHANCELLOR AT WAGNER LEADERSHIP INSTITUTE

In this amazing book, my dear friend Kris Vallotton encourages us that in order to love our neighbors we must love ourselves and care for our own souls. We are made for community and he urges us that we can't reach our full potential until we surround ourselves with covenant friends who share our DNA. I often say I have the best team in the world but I hope other leaders would argue with me on that. I pray that as you read this you will be inspired to partner with others, dream big in God, and spread His love throughout this world as beloved sons and daughters. You are called to shine for Jesus and you are destined to win!

—HEIDI G. BAKER, PHD, COFOUNDER AND CEO OF IRIS GLOBAL

Kris Vallotton's passion for seeing people fully alive and totally equipped for success comes across loud and clear on every page of this new book. Kris leads readers on a journey to discover their God-given identity in order to fulfill their Kingdom purpose. What could be more important than that? This is a must-read for anyone who desires to be an instrument of transformation!

—Dr. Ed Silvoso, founder of Harvest Evangelism/Transform Our World

What you are about to read on the pages of *Destined to Win* will change your life. This book is filled with brilliant insights, supernatural wisdom, and stories that will inspire you to personal greatness. But greatness from God's perspective has little to do with power, money, or fame. His design for us has to do with the freedom to dream, while fulfilling our God-given purpose. Kris Vallotton has captured the heart of God on this subject, largely through his own personal journey. One of the greatest miracles I've ever seen has been the miracle of God's grace at work in this man who truly has a heart after God. His hunger, humility, and willingness to sacrifice all has brought him to a place of personal breakthrough. It is beautiful to watch. Reading this book will give you a glimpse into your own victorious destiny, for all of us are destined to win.

—Bill Johnson, pastor of Bethel Church in Redding, CA and author of *When Heaven Invades Earth* and *God is Good*

Destined to Win was created from Kris's own vulnerable process as well as some masterly thought through principles. I love how everything Kris writes imparts identity but this book also imparts wisdom through emotional intelligence over your own journey. He creates steps about finding your people, boarding the right bus, and creating a personal connection to many principles you have heard before but are now presented in ways that you can apply to your own success. Bottom line: Kris has a unique way of imparting wisdom that helps you reign in life. I so appreciated his latest work and I know you will as well!

—Shawn Bolz, TV host and pastor of bolzministries.com and author of *Translating God, Keys to Heaven's Economy,* and *Growing Up With God*

King Solomon said, "the writing of many books is endless." The psalmist said, "Let this be written for the next generation, for a people not yet born, that they may praise the Lord." Once again, Kris Vallotton uses his unique ability to combine transparency, vulnerability, and experience to produce distilled wisdom to teach powerful truths that make *Destined To Win* a practical manual for survival and success. In some ways it's late—we could have used it two decades ago; in other ways, it's right on time—the Church desperately needs these principles; and yet in other ways—it speaks to that generation yet to be born who will cling to its words because of the promise of life it conveys.

—Bishop Joseph L. Garlington Sr., senior pastor
of Covenant Church of Pittsburgh

Destined
to Win

OTHER BOOKS BY KRIS VALLOTTON

Supernatural Ways of Royalty

Basic Training for the Supernatural Ways of Royalty

Developing a Supernatural Lifestyle

Basic Training for the Prophetic Ministry

Moral Revolution

Heavy Rain

40 Day Journey to Purity for Guys

40 Day Journey to Purity for Girls

Supernatural Power of Forgiveness

Spirit Wars

Outrageous Courage

Fashioned to Reign

The Ways of Royalty (Children's Book)

School of the Prophets

Destined to Win

HOW TO EMBRACE YOUR GOD-GIVEN IDENTITY
AND REALIZE YOUR KINGDOM PURPOSE

KRIS VALLOTTON

NELSON
BOOKS

An Imprint of Thomas Nelson

Published in Nashville, Tennessee, by Nelson Books, an imprint of Thomas Nelson. Nelson Books and Thomas Nelson are registered trademarks of HarperCollins Christian Publishing, Inc.

Published in association with the literary agency of The FEDD Agency, Inc., P.O. Box 341973, Austin, Texas, 78734.

Thomas Nelson titles may be purchased in bulk for educational, business, fund-raising, or sales promotional use. For information, please e-mail SpecialMarkets@ThomasNelson.com.

Any Internet addresses, phone numbers, or company or product information printed in this book are offered as a resource and are not intended in any way to be or to imply an endorsement by Thomas Nelson, nor does Thomas Nelson vouch for the existence, content, or services of these sites, phone numbers, companies, or products beyond the life of this book.

Unless otherwise noted, Scripture quotations are taken from New American Standard Bible˚, Copyright © 1960, 1962, 1963, 1968, 1971, 1972, 1973, 1975, 1977, 1995 by The Lockman Foundation. Used by permission. (www.Lockman.org). Scripture quotations marked KJV are from the King James Version. Scripture quotations marked THE MESSAGE are from *The Message*. Copyright © by Eugene H. Peterson 1993, 1994, 1995, 1996, 2000, 2001, 2002. Used by permission of NavPress. All rights reserved. Represented by Tyndale House Publishers, Inc. Scripture quotations marked NIV are from the Holy Bible, New International Version˚, NIV˚. Copyright © 1973, 1978, 1984, 2011 by Biblica, Inc.˜ Used by permission of Zondervan. All rights reserved worldwide. www.zondervan.com. The "NIV" and "New International Version" are trademarks registered in the United States Patent and Trademark Office by Biblica, Inc.˜ Scripture quotations marked NKJV are from the New King James Version˚. © 1982 by Thomas Nelson. Used by permission. All rights reserved.

Library of Congress Cataloging-in-Publication Data

Names: Vallotton, Kris, author.
Title: Destined to win: how to embrace your God-given identity and realize your kingdom purpose / Kris Vallotton.
Description: Nashville, Tennessee: Nelson Books, an imprint of Thomas Nelson, [2017]
Identifiers: LCCN 2016036955 | ISBN 9780718080648
Subjects: LCSH: Success—Religious aspects—Christianity. | Self-actualization (Psychology)—Religious aspects—Christianity. | Identity (Psychology)—Religious aspects—Christianity. | Vocation—Christianity.
Classification: LCC BV4598.3 .V355 2017 | DDC 248.4—dc23 LC record available at https://lccn.loc.gov/2016036955

Printed in the United States of America

17 18 19 20 21 RRD 6 5 4 3

I dedicate *Destined to Win* to my mother who lost her husband, the man of her dreams, when she was twenty years young. Alone with two small children and a broken heart, she forged her way through life with amazing kindness and intense perseverance. In the years that followed, tragedy and hardship would continue to hang over our family like a thick black cloud; yet my mother remained a bright light shining through the darkness.

My mother's incredible love has carried me through the worst situations, and her faith in me remains the driving force in the core of my being. She is the angel on my shoulder, the cheerleader in my corner, and my friend in the storms of life. She makes me laugh when I am low, reminds me of who I am when I have lost my way, and is the loudest voice in my victories.

I love you, Mama! You were the first one to ever believe in me, and you taught me that I was destined to win!

Contents

Foreword

"Have I not commanded you? Be strong and courageous.
Do not be afraid; do not be discouraged, for the Lord
your God will be with you wherever you go."

JOSHUA 1:9 NLT

Everywhere I look I see people being crushed under the weight of discouragement. It's so clear that the enemy is using this as a weapon to keep many of us from wholeheartedly following God, which is exactly why *Destined to Win* is such an important message. Within these pages, my friend Kris shares the trials and challenges he's encountered in his own life to help us recognize that God is bigger than any situation we may face. He encourages us to understand that if we allow Jesus to walk with us, we cannot fail. Making a habit of remembering the times God has come through for us is such a significant strategy for fighting the discouragement that threatens to ensnare us! Like Kris, we can all think of times in our past when God showed up for us right when we were about to give up. Time and time again, God makes something beautiful out of our dark situations. Just as Kris lends hope to us by sharing the victories of God in his own life, we too should make a habit of remembering and sharing how the Lord has worked on our behalf. This remembrance stirs our faith and empowers us to face trials with courage and tenacity, knowing that God will be our victory again!

I encourage you to dive into this book with expectation and excitement. Buckle up for a fun and wild ride with Kris, from the day he drove off as a confused teenager in a smoke-spewing, rusted-out '57 Ford Fairlane nicknamed *Captain America*, to the glorious mountaintops of seeing God birth the world-changing ministry of the Bethel School of Supernatural Ministry.

And together, let's remember: when we encounter hard times, we need only lift our gaze to heaven, believe in the grace of the One who has saved us, and know that with Him, we are destined to win.

—LISA BEVERE
Messenger International, bestselling author of
Without Rival, Lioness Arising, and *Girls with Swords*

INTRODUCTION

The world is filled with amazing people who are walking in their divine callings, changing history, and seeing their dreams come true. They have discovered their true identities, harnessed their strengths, focused their energies, and maximized their opportunities. Successful people know how to love well; they lead passionate, productive lives. When they fail (and everyone does), they learn from their mistakes and gain wisdom to rise to new heights with God and in life.

Successful people make the most out of these opportunities and thereby profoundly impact the world around them. When life gives them lemons, they make lemonade; and when things get tough they grow stronger. They refuse to become victims because they know they were born to be winners . . . victors . . . champions!

Yet other remarkable people, for various reasons, find themselves waiting for life to begin. These people sit daily at the porch of possibility, eating their Lucky Charms while longing to be discovered. They each pray for a big break, dream of a better life, and hope for a deeper love. Like a beautiful bird that has wings but never learns to fly, they see life as a well of untapped potential, a buried chest filled with secret treasures waiting to be unearthed.

The truth is, no matter where you find yourself in life, there is always more: more things to learn, more people to help, and more obstacles to overcome. I long to see people fully actualized in a way that causes them to embrace their God-given identities and fulfill their divine purposes. My heart yearns to see people become fully alive and totally equipped: His story-makers, who alter the course of history toward God's incredible kingdom!

In 1997 I became so overcome with the desire to equip people for their divine purposes that I left our four businesses and our home in the woods to join the Bethel Church leadership team. That same year, Bill Johnson and I (along with our amazing team) founded the Bethel School of Ministry in Redding, California. The school quickly became a catalyst for people who wanted to rewrite their personal stories and grab hold of the callings God had for their lives; it grew to more than two thousand students (in a city of less than ninety thousand) in just seventeen years. In fact, the school grew so large and so fast that we soon found ourselves completely out of room. In 2001 we added another wing to our building, but it was full before we finished it. The word continued to spread, and people kept coming from all over the planet. Before long we found ourselves stretched all around the city in several different buildings; in spite of the inconvenience, more students continued to enroll with passion in their eyes and fire in their hearts.

In 2012 BSM took over the Redding Civic Auditorium (the largest auditorium in our county) to house just half of our student body. As of this writing we are again out of room, necessitating one of the largest building projects in the history of our city. The school now trains nearly nine hundred international students annually. People all over the world are so hungry to reach their full potential in God that their passions have caused BSM to become the largest international SEVIS-certified (U.S. Immigration and Customs Enforcement–certified) vocational school in America.

As I travel the world, I have discovered that, despite the incredible growth we've seen already, there are still so many more people who long to have the same experiences our students are having; yet for a variety of reasons, they can't make the journey. This book is my attempt to speak to that need, to capture some of the most remarkable things we have learned about calling and purpose over the last two decades for those who haven't been able to make it to Redding.

I'm personally inviting you to join me on this journey as we venture to uncover the buried treasure hidden in the hearts of every reader. My goal is that all who brave the pages of this manuscript will become fully alive, passionate people who learn the secrets of success in God and become equipped to apprehend their divine purpose in life.

After two decades of equipping people, I have come to realize there is no such thing as a magic pill or overnight success in God. But as thousands of our students would attest, there is a common process that prepares us for the actualization of our dreams. Let me be clear: I am not naïve enough to believe that everyone who reads this book will experience a transformed life, but I do believe that most everyone can learn enough to dramatically impact his or her life and ultimately have a positive effect on the kingdom of God.

As you join me on this expedition, I want to challenge you to posture yourself for change. My prayer is that God would meet you in the pages of this book and cause *all* of His dreams for you to come true. You are destined to win!

1

CAPTAIN AMERICA

Henry was my best friend in high school. He was a short, stocky kid who sort of walked like a duck. His parents forced him to go to church, so he spent most of his growing-up years trying to escape the religious stigma that plagued him. I was a tall, skinny kid (five feet eleven, 137 pounds) who practiced my "cool walk" at home, strutting as if I had a stick up my butt! We were such a pair.

We both longed to be accepted by the popular crowd, and we did everything we could to fit in. We cussed and acted mean. I even wore skinny jeans and white T-shirts, but Henry's wardrobe was a medley of thrift-shop finds. His mom did her best to dress him "nice," but Henry's mismatched and outdated clothes only added to the kid's misfortune. The truth is that his parents really loved and cared for him, but they were Flintstones . . . out of touch with the real world.

Henry grew up on the poor side of town, just down the street from a wrecking yard. This became his hangout, an escape from a world of brokenness. He quickly became somewhat of a junkyard dog and gofer all wrapped up in one dirty, greasy kid. When Henry was finally old enough to have a driver's license, the yard boss let him rescue a tired, rusted-out '57 Ford Fairlane from the crusher before they smashed the thing. This diamond in the rough was originally painted a two-tone white and salmon color, but it had faded to a kind of ugly pink, which came off on your clothes whenever you rubbed up against it.

The first week after Henry rescued the car from the yard it was obvious to both of us that it needed some serious upgrades! First things first, we took it to our auto shop class and sprayed the entire outside with about ten cans of gray primer. Then, in flat black, we stenciled the words *Captain America* in huge letters on both sides of the car. After that, we put the junker up on the lift and drilled holes in the mufflers so it would sound like a race car.

The seats were so ripped up that the stuffing was falling out onto the floorboards, so we bought about three rolls of duct tape and reupholstered the seats with it. The only down side was that you had to be careful when sliding into the car, because the duct tape would stick your butt to the seat, not to mention the fact that getting the glue off your jeans was almost impossible.

The aesthetics definitely needed some work, but the ride was also in need of serious help. One of the many unique qualities of Captain America was its ability to burn almost as much oil as it did gasoline. Whenever we would stop at a red light and rev the engine, blueish smoke would completely cover the car. Henry called it the "glory cloud."

The truth is, we thought that heap was really cool, but looking back now I can see we were the laughingstocks of our school. Let's just say that none of the ladies wanted a ride home.

What Henry and I didn't understand back then was that stenciling *Captain America* on the side of the car didn't make us superheroes any more than drilling holes in the mufflers made that piece of junk a race car. Duct tape may be fine to seal HVAC connection points, but it certainly wasn't designed to upholster seats. We were just two young boys desperately trying to fit in . . . to be loved . . . to be known. We thought the world was laughing *with* us; we had no idea the world was laughing *at* us.

The reality was that Henry and I were never going to fit in; we weren't good at anything the cool crowd valued. More important, we didn't like ourselves. I understand now that Captain America was more than an automobile; it was an outward manifestation of our inward brokenness. Our lives were duct-taped together because our dysfunctional families had beaten the stuffing out of us. It was all we could do to keep our intense pain from leaking out of our ears. We painted over the faded glory of our boyhoods, but we couldn't cover the discolored, rusted-out, painful years of rejection. We stenciled *Captain America* on our T-shirts, but there were still two scared little boys under the hood. We roared like race cars coming down the street, talking tough and cussing like sailors; yet it was all smoke and mirrors: a low-budget film with poor actors and no plot. Our self-hatred bonded us together; we fed one another's brokenness and provided a generic intimacy for our starving souls. We were just two blind boys stumbling through the darkness, grasping for acceptance, and longing for love.

The world is filled with people like Henry and Kris who survive in the painful existence of symptomatic cures, reactionary lifestyles, and loveless cultures. They flock together, validating one another's dysfunction, measuring their level of achievement (or lack of it) by comparing themselves to one another. An ancient Israelite prophet named Isaiah put it this way: "All of us like sheep have gone astray" (Isaiah 53:6).

But, as most of you know, we are not powerless victims! In fact, we were born to win. We don't have eyes in the backs of our heads because we weren't designed to back up, retreat, or lose ground. Furthermore, our arms were created to only work in front of us, building what's before us. Our feet point forward and are incapable of swiveling rearward, making retreat a slow, difficult process. It's all a sign of our Creator's desire for us to gain ground and to live successful, productive lives. God is our rear guard, and we are to face forward.

Knowing this, how are we to move ahead, to become prosperous in the Kingdom? We must discover our true identities, proactively develop noble virtues, and get to the root causes of our destructive and/or unproductive behaviors. We have to take off our masks and refuse to live a photoshopped life! It's imperative that we wake up to the stunning reality of God's superior kingdom, while learning how to navigate this journey we call life. We are called to greatness and destined for glory.

> GOD IS OUR REAR GUARD, AND WE ARE TO FACE FORWARD.

Greatness Defined

Greatness and *fame* are terms often confused or even used interchangeably. Fame is usually the result of some popular act: a ball is caught, a song is sung, a book is written, or a character is played. But greatness cannot be reduced to an action or an event. Kingdom greatness is measured long after the crowds have dispersed, the applause has silenced, and the stage lights have cooled, because true greatness lies deep in the heart of every person. In fact, genuine greatness is most often exposed in the dark times, in the secret places, and in the alone hours of a believer's existence. It is in these desert seasons that the seedbeds of God's greatness, the attributes we need to cultivate, are conceived. It is later—often much later—that the results are revealed to the world.

The Scriptures describe men and women of God who cultivated these qualities and took hold of their positions of divine influence to shift the destinies of nations. Their prominence was not for their own benefit, but for the purpose of shaping society toward God's original intent. They created catalytic cultures that maximized the godly influence of their constituents on the rest of creation. Believers throughout the book of Acts are great examples of noble people who catalyzed culture. They had such deep impacts on their societies that when Paul and his friends arrived in Thessalonica, the people said, "These who have turned the world upside down have come here too" (Acts 17:6 NKJV).

The world is crying out for people like Paul—and Joseph—who will become fathers and mothers to the pharaohs of the world (see Genesis 45) and see whole nations fall into the hands of the Lord. God is summoning the Daniels of the earth who can stand as he did in the courts of four worldly kings and bring the most powerful nations into the Kingdom. God is gathering the Nehemiahs of our day to rebuild our ruined cities and restore hope to the planet. He is awakening the Davids of our generation and commissioning them to defeat the giants of racism, crime, immorality, and corruption that seem to roam the earth wreaking havoc on our children.

This is our moment, our time, our Jordan River crossing, our season for epic transition. We are God's X factor, His secret weapon, His ace in the hole, His divine strategy for global reformation. That's right. We are the "salt of the earth" (Matthew 5:13). We preserve the planet and are vital to life in the Kingdom.

We are the light rising in the darkness that is longing for a new day to dawn. It's you and me, and it's people like us all over the world who are taking hold of this mandate to stand firm in our stations at the height of every city and shine against the backdrop of doom. Together we are the "light of the world" (Matthew 5:14), illuminating breathtaking solutions to people in desperate, despairing, and destructive circumstances.

The teacher in Proverbs, as he encouraged his students to pursue wisdom instead of folly, told them,

> The LORD by wisdom founded the earth,
> By understanding He established the heavens.
> By His knowledge the deeps were broken up
> And the skies drip with dew.
>
> (PROVERBS 3:19–20)

It was wisdom that formed the earth, and it is wisdom that will reform it. When explaining to his readers that God's grace made him a preacher to the Gentiles so that His church would grow, the apostle Paul concluded that "the manifold wisdom of God might now be made known through the church to the rulers and the authorities in the heavenly places" (Ephesians 3:10). God used Paul to deliver His gospel to the Gentile church; now that church broadcasts His wisdom to the rest of creation. Each of us who follows Jesus is endowed with the wisdom of God. It is His wisdom in us that is about to be demonstrated through us to the rulers around us, to restore the earth beneath us, so that His city above us can be the habitation among us.

That's who you are, and that's who I am! We are sons and daughters of the King, filled with wisdom and living in His radiance. This is not a fantasy or some script from a superhero movie. It's the truth that frees the world to fulfill the Creator's original intentions, our divine design, our Master's mandate.

2

FROM THE INSIDE OUT

If you asked most people who Norma Jeane Mortenson was, they probably wouldn't know. Yet nearly everyone in America has heard of Marilyn Monroe. Marilyn's real name was Norma Jeane Mortenson. Her mother was a film cutter at RKO Studios who, abandoned by her husband, spent most of her life in and out of mental institutions. As a result, Marilyn spent a large portion of her childhood abused and alone, trapped inside the foster care system.

Battered but not broken, Marilyn quickly worked her way to superstardom. By the time she hit her early thirties, Marilyn had become one of the most desired women in all of Hollywood; however, this was short-lived.

Marilyn wrote, "Hollywood is a place where they'll pay you a thousand dollars for a kiss and fifty cents for your soul."[1] Her words are sobering and reveal a dark side to our performance-driven society that creates its heroes from the outside in.

Maybe this is the reason why most of us spend so long getting ready for each day. We shower, fix our hair, brush our teeth, and do the best we can to look beautiful on the outside, yet we rarely give any thought to enhancing the souls within us. The fixation we have with impressing one another has led to the adage, "Beauty is only skin deep, but ugly goes all the way to the bone." When external beauty is a manifestation of the healthy soul that lies within you, it feels authentic, real, and attractive. But when the soul within you is drowning, starving, ignored, and unkempt, everything you do on the outside is futile. Such was the case with Marilyn.

> WHEN EXTERNAL BEAUTY IS A MANIFESTATION OF THE HEALTHY SOUL THAT LIES WITHIN YOU, IT FEELS AUTHENTIC, REAL, AND ATTRACTIVE.

Marilyn never quite made it out of the hell into which she was born. Rich, and yet miserable, she overdosed on barbiturates at just thirty-six years old; this was the heartbreaking tragedy of living as Marilyn Monroe on the outside when all the while Norma Jeane remained within.

In His Sermon on the Mount, Jesus warned crowds of listeners about this type of living. He used the word *hypocrite*, which comes from the Greek word *hypokrite*, meaning "stage actors" (Matthew 6:5, 16). He compared scribes and Pharisees to clean-looking cups filled with selfishness and to clean, beautiful tombs full of unclean, dead bones (Matthew 23:25–27); He compared

false prophets to ravenous wolves dressed up a
7:15).

We see these words in the Bible and want to distance
from scribes, Pharisees, and false prophets, but the worris
truth is that this same problem infects our lives, too, in ways we
may not clearly see. Many self-help books today are more like
acting lessons that teach people how to behave in the big-screen
movie of life; but if we're honest with ourselves, we'll see that the
training they impart is just spray paint and stenciling for anyone
hoping to become like Captain America. It rarely ends well.

It's incumbent upon us to ask the question, why do we pretend? I think it's because we are all born with an intense need to
feel significant, loved, valued, and accepted; yet we fear that we
are not worthy of these things. So we pretend to be the people we
think society wants us to be in order to meet the desperate needs
of our souls.

Let me be clear: these are not just wants or desires; these are
God-given needs. What water, food, air, sleep, and sunlight are to
your body; love, acceptance, attention, approval, and significance
are to your soul.

Sadly, most believers don't even acknowledge, much less
manage, these needs because they were actually taught by their
pastors to ignore their souls! In fact, in many circles the soul is
thought of as something inherently evil. In other words, some
people teach that to be truly spiritual you must suppress or ignore
the needs of your soul and instead focus only on spiritual things.

If a person is drowning in a pool, nobody stands by and says,
"You need air, you airless person! If you would just read your
Bible more often, you wouldn't need air!" We all know that no

natter how spiritual somebody is, he or she still needs air. You can go to church every day, read your Bible consistently, and pray all the time, but none of these things will fulfill the need you have for oxygen.

John struck at the heart of this issue when he wrote to encourage his friend and follower Gaius, "Beloved, I pray that in all respects you may prosper and be in good health, just as your soul prospers" (3 John 2). Did you notice that prosperity and health are directly related to your soul and not your spirit? Sunday after Sunday, all around the world, people are taught how to become more spiritual, but we never teach them how to manage their souls. But if all prosperity and health are directly related to our souls, and only indirectly related to our spirits, it's imperative that we first acknowledge and then manage the needs of our souls. Otherwise, we will find ourselves drowning in the sea of humanity, starving for love, affection, acceptance, significance, attention, and approval.

Tridimensional Wholeness

Acts 3 tells the story of Peter and John going to the temple at 3:00 p.m. to pray. There was a man there who had been born lame, and he was begging for money. Peter basically said, "We don't have money because we are ministers, but what we do have we will gladly give to you. In the name of Jesus, walk!" Then Peter grabbed the guy by the hand and lifted him up.

Suddenly the guy jumped up and started walking, leaping, and praising God. In other words, he was healed physically (walking), he was healed emotionally (leaping: a physical mani-festation of excitement or joy), and he was healed spiritually (praising God)! It's a beautiful demonstration of the tridimen-sional nature of God, because God heals the whole man (Acts 3:1–8).

The next verses, though, are quite disheartening. They read, "All the people saw him *walking* and *praising* God; . . . and they were filled with wonder and amazement at what had happened to him" (3:9–10, emphasis added). Did you catch that huge omis-sion? The guy *leaped*, but the people only noticed his walking and praising! I mean, the man had a tridimensional encounter with Jesus, yet the cultural value system blinded these people to a massive portion of the guy's miracle. He was emotionally healed, and nobody caught it. The soul was lost in the shuffle as it so often is, even today.

What Went Wrong

One of the major reasons we devalue the soul is a misunderstand-ing of a single passage in the book of Hebrews. It reads, "For the word of God is living and active and sharper than any two-edged sword, and piercing as far as the division of soul and spirit, of both joints and marrow, and able to judge the thoughts and intentions of the heart" (Hebrews 4:12).

At first glance the verse seems to be saying the Lord wants to separate the soul from the spirit, the spirit being good and the soul being evil.

Harold Eberle helped to clear this up for me. Harold is a

Greek scholar who says that a more accurate rendering of the original text would read: "For the word of God is living and active and sharper than any two edged sword, and piercing as far as the division between soul and soul, and spirit and spirit, of both joints and marrow, and able to judge the thoughts and intentions of the heart."[2]

In other words, instead of the sword dividing between the soul and the spirit, the sword is actually dividing the soul from the soul and the spirit from the spirit. What does this mean, you ask? It's a beautiful picture of sanctification in which God uses His Word (depicted as a sword) to separate what shouldn't be in your soul from what should be and what shouldn't be in your spirit from what should be. God's sword is so sharp He can cut out every single cell that shouldn't be in your soul and remove every single cell that shouldn't be in your spirit, all without harming one divinely placed cell in your being!

Soul Needs

We must learn to care for our soul needs if we ever hope to cultivate Kingdom virtues that empower us to walk in our high callings. When the body of Christ devalues the soul and declares it irrelevant or, worse yet, believes it's evil, then the needs of the soul are never proactively met. This creates a soul desert where people passionately pursue mirages, illusions emerging out of the dry heat of an affectionless community.

Mirages are not the result of someone's willful actions; instead they are the unhealthy side effects of dehydration. I love this addage: "A full man dislikes honey, but to a famished man any bitter thing is sweet" (Proverbs 27:7, paraphrase mine).

Soul-desert cultures use certain phrases to condemn the manifestations of their people's soul needs, effectively communicating the conviction that the needs of the inner man are to be ignored, or even denied. Here are a few of the most common ones: "That person is in the flesh!" "They just want attention!" "They're just trying to get people to like them!" "They just need to feel like they're important!" "That person is so clingy!"

Yes, that person is in the flesh, but even Jesus was the Word that became flesh and dwelled among us (John 1:1, 14). And the apostle Paul said, "Husbands ought also to love their own wives as their own bodies. He who loves his own wife loves himself; for no one ever hated his own flesh, but nourishes and cherishes it, just as Christ also does the church" (Ephesians 5:28–29).

"Kris," you ask, "are you saying that I am supposed to feed and value my flesh?"

No, the apostle Paul said that! I'm simply repeating what the Bible says. You should take care of the needs of your natural man, because your body is the temple of the Holy Spirit. Likewise, your soul was created in the image of God, and it also requires intentional care. Can you say, "paradigm shift"?

Soul Power

David, the man after God's own heart, was extraordinarily in touch with the needs of his soul, and consequently his soul loved God. Look at the way David talked to his soul:

> Why are you in despair, O my soul?
> And why have you become disturbed within me?
> Hope in God, for I shall again praise Him
> For the help of His presence.
>
> (PSALM 42:5)

David wrote this after he escaped from Abimelech:

> My soul will make its boast in the LORD;
> The humble will hear it and rejoice.
>
> (PSALM 34:2)

After a time of deep distress, David's soul was bragging about the Lord!

Even when he is wandering in a literal desert, David has soul-ish ways:

> O God, You are my God; I shall seek You earnestly;
> My soul thirsts for You, my flesh yearns for You,
> In a dry and weary land where there is no water.
>
> (PSALM 63:1)

Did you catch that? David's soul hungered for God, and the guy wasn't even born again! There are hundreds of references to the soul of David loving on God.

Of course the most famous soul quote is in Psalm 23, and yet we often miss the best verse in this passage. David proclaimed, "[The LORD] restores my soul" (v. 3). Yes! This is just like the story of the man at the temple gate. You know the guy: the lame man who leaped. This is it. This is what we all need! We need to be whole on the inside, so we can be real on the outside. No more pretenders. No more Captain America wannabes. No more stage actors!

Check out what Moses heard, straight from the mouth of God. The Lord said, "You shall love the LORD your God with all your heart and with all your *soul* and with all your might" (Deuteronomy 6:5, emphasis added). There it is again, but this time it is God exhorting His people to have a tridimensional relationship with Him. It's simple and yet profound, isn't it? Love God with all your heart (the Old Testament word for *spirit*), with all your soul, and with all your might (body).

We should all have a tridimensional plan for our tridimensional beings, so that we can walk, leap, and praise God. It's only through a healthy, whole being that the Kingdom can be accurately expressed to the world around you. In the process you will become a fully actualized, completely alive child of the King.

I won't cover too much of the "walking" and "praising God" dimensions of your being in this book. It certainly is important to take care of your body and to live a physically healthy life, but that discussion is beyond the scope of this book for two reasons: (1) there are hundreds of books written on the subject, and (2) there are people who are far more qualified than I am to address these essential topics.

> IT'S ONLY THROUGH A HEALTHY, WHOLE BEING THAT THE KINGDOM CAN BE ACCURATELY EXPRESSED TO THE WORLD AROUND YOU.

Neither will I dive too deeply into the spiritual side of life, at least not in the traditional way it's been taught in churches. I have written four other books dealing with the subject of growing your spirit man and embracing the power of the spirit.[3] In the following pages, however, we will dig deeper into what it means to "leap" . . . to love and care for your soul. Let's begin by discussing the various ways you can meet the needs of your soul.

Three Ways to Live

There are three main ways we tend to approach meeting the needs of our souls: inactively, reactively, or proactively.

You are *inactive* when you remain ignorant of the condition of your soul. In the inactive mind-set you embrace your desperate need as an unwanted yet necessary part of life's process. Then you work hard to convince yourself that love, acceptance, attention, approval, and significance are not necessities but choices that can be opted out of. Maybe you don't try to meet the needs of your soul because you want to be spiritual, so you wear your dysfunction as a badge of honor. Or worse yet, you bury your needs so deep that you can't consciously remember where you even put them. Life just happens to you when you live inactively. Eventually, you find your soul existing in brokenness, emptiness, and loneliness.

You are *reactive* when you acknowledge your soul's needs but then fulfill the needs in dysfunctional ways. This is the proverbial "looking for love in all the wrong places" scenario. Living reactively often leads to all kinds of extremely dysfunctional devices that never fulfill your need to be known deeply or your desire to be loved for who you are. The fruit of this reactive life-style may be sexual promiscuity, pornography, fantasy, selfish ambition, and so on . . . anything that gives you the sense of being known, feeling powerful, and feeling loved. Yet instant gratification has horrible side effects! Typically people who live this way for any length of time have a trail full of broken relationships that follow them.

You are *proactive* when you wisely assess the needs of your soul and then devise a healthy strategy to meet your needs. Metaphorically speaking, you stop eating out of dumpsters, and you start planning your meals.

One of the most basic ways to do this is through the power of love. You need a deep understanding and acceptance of love to seep so powerfully into your soul that it overflows out of you and into the hearts of others.

Love Is All You Need?

Let's visit some of the foundational ways that *felt* love affects your soul and look into some healthy ways to proactively experience this kind of love.

In some ways it's true that "all you need is love," especially when you examine the Bible's definitions of love. So let's take a close look at the love of God—its definitions, attributes, expressions, and outcomes.

LOVE EXPERIENCED

I am convinced that wars would cease, crime would plummet, divorce would diminish, and immorality would fall if the human race just experienced these three words: you are loved!

When I first came to Bethel Church, one of my primary roles was counseling. I counseled about six people a day, four days a week, for about three years. Most of the people I worked with would identify themselves as Christians. Nearly all of them could quote (and often would quote) John 3:16, which reads, "For God so loved the world, that He gave His only begotten Son . . ." But I rarely met with people who had actually experienced the love of God. They stored truth in their heads, but somehow it never made the eighteen-inch journey to their hearts.

I am convinced that your heart can take you places your head can never go! The teacher in Proverbs put it like this:

> Trust in the LORD with all your heart
> And do not lean on your own understanding.
> (PROVERBS 3:5)

Did you notice the wisest man in the world clearly said that we must trust God with our hearts, not our heads? In fact, he went on to say that we shouldn't put a lot of weight in what we understand.

This is a difficult idea for those of us from Western cultures to process. In fact, there are two lies related to this dichotomy between the heart and the head that keep Westerners from experiencing the love of God. The first one is, "If we can explain God's love, then we understand it. And if we understand it, we have experienced it." The second lie is worse. It says, "We can't experience something until we understand it."

First of all, I would like to point out there is no definition of romantic love (much less God's love) that adequately explains the experience. Furthermore, not one of us has ever fallen in love by reading the dictionary definitions of passion, romance, or love! Definitions pale in light of the experience.

Love was redefined for me the day I met Kathy lying on a raft in the middle of a lake in Nice, California. That girl took my breath away! I couldn't sleep, I wasn't hungry, and I couldn't think. I was in love, and passion was awakened in me! There was no way I could explain what I was experiencing, but I certainly tried. I would spend hours talking to anybody who would listen to me as I tried desperately to explain the love I felt for Kathy. As you might imagine, the only people who understood me were those who themselves had the same experience. If romantic, human love has to be experienced to be understood, then how can the love of God be explained before it's experienced?

Second, if the love of God must be experienced to be explained, then it stands to reason that you can experience things (and often do) before you can explain them. Believing you've experienced love because you have a biblical definition of it—or because you've memorized all the verses about the love of God in the Bible—is not only deceptive, it's also destructive. Think about it: why would you continue to press in to experience deeper levels of God's love if you're convinced that there is nothing more to experience beyond the definition? In other words, what you know can keep you from what you need to know. This is especially true if you are unconsciously ignorant. You don't know that you don't know!

Just what are we missing when we limit our experience of God's love to the definition we think we understand?

The apostle Paul prayed for the church that "[the Father] would grant you . . . to be strengthened with power through His Spirit in the inner man, so that Christ may dwell in your hearts through faith; and that you, being rooted and grounded in love, may be able to comprehend with all the saints what is the breadth and length and height and depth, and to know the love of Christ which surpasses knowledge, that you may be filled up to all the fullness of God" (Ephesians 3:16–19).

Oh man, that's a mouthful! Did you feel it? Did you see it? Did you get it? Wow! Three things stand out to me from this passage: First of all, we are supposed to be rooted and grounded in love. In other words, the core foundation of everything we believe, do, say, live, and experience must flow from love, be motivated by love, and be grounded in love. And we are not to be rooted and grounded in just any love, but in the *agape* love of God that must be experienced to be comprehended (*agape* is the Greek word for God's love).

But wait, it gets better! You are also invited to comprehend the love of God that's beyond comprehension. Check it out one more time: "to know the love of Christ which surpasses knowledge." This is the place where the infinite transcends the finite, the supernatural infuses the biological, and the heart is enlightened to the secret dimensions of His passion for you! You heard me right; He is wild about you! He didn't just die for you; He lives for you. In fact, He lives in you, around you, and through you.

God is all about you! I don't mean you are all He has; I just mean you are His favorite. He tells you secrets the angels wish they knew (1 Peter 1:12). You are God's inheritance (Ephesians 1:18); you are His son or daughter—His child—and part of His cosmic family (Romans 8:12–25). You are the only creature ever made in His image and likeness (Genesis 1:26), the only one to be redeemed by the death of God Himself (John 3:16), and the only one allowed to carry His glory (John 17:22). You are the apple of His eye (Zechariah 2:8), the hope of His glory (Colossians 1:27), and the bride of the Bridegroom (Revelation 21:2). God rejoices over you with shouts of joy (Zephaniah 3:17). No one and nothing can separate you from His love (Romans 8:38–39), and anyone who messes with you must answer to Him (Romans 8:31).

I can't tell you how many times I've watched people crumble under the revelation of God's love for them. Often, in the midst of counseling people, I have told them that they need to experience the love of the Father. This must be some sort of unwritten signal for them to unleash a torrent of Bible verses because, almost without fail, believers feel compelled to quote every verse they have ever memorized from the Bible on the subject of love. When their surge subsides, I usually quietly lay my hand on their shoulders and ask the Father to show them His love. The responses are often dramatic and shocking. I've observed several of them falling out of their chairs onto the floor as waves of the Father's love encompassed them. Others laughed uncontrollably for hours as God revealed layers and layers of His love for them.

It's amazing to witness the healing power of God's love. One story that catches my breath is about a girl I will call Jane. Jane was a pastor's daughter who grew up in a fairly healthy home, but she had a serious case of anorexia. From the time she was thirteen years old, she spent more than half of her life in the hospital, often on life support. She nearly died four times. She had just been released from the hospital when I met her in a church service during a conference. She was about twenty years old then; she was very beautiful, yet she was skin and bones. Evidently her parents had begged her to come and hear me speak. Fear and shame had imprisoned Jane's soul and relegated her to the walls of her bedroom, but she had left the safety of home to come to church that day.

She was sitting up front right next to me, although I had no idea who she was. During worship I suddenly felt prompted to lean over to this frail young woman and tell her how much God loved her. At first she seemed resistant, even defiant, but I persisted. I asked her if I could pray for her. In a quiet, shaky voice she said, "I guess so."

I put my hand on her shoulder and began to pray a simple prayer over and over. "Jesus, show this beautiful woman how much you love her," I asked. At first nothing seemed to change on the outside, but I could sense her heart softening, so I continued to pray. "Jesus, show this beautiful woman how much you love her!"

Tears emerged from her eyes and rolled gently down her face. Seconds later she fell to the ground in a puddle of tears, as her gentle weeping turned to violent sobbing.

I decided to leave her alone and let Jesus love on her. For a couple of hours she laid on the floor while waves of Jesus' love crashed over her soul and washed her clean. Shame and guilt seemed to evaporate in the sunlight of God's intense love. Most of the story was written in Jane's countenance as she emerged from the puddle on the floor.

It's been four years now since Jane was touched by the love

of God. Since then she's graduated from three years of the Bethel School of Ministry, she's completely free of anorexia, and she is living a normal, healthy life.

The incredible thing is that Jane's story is not unique! I have witnessed thousands of people touched by the extravagant love of God, freed from the bondage of sin, released from the prison of addictions, and healed in the depths of their souls. This is what happens when the revelation of Jesus' love makes the eighteen-inch journey from the head to the heart. This is love experienced and yet not explained. This is it!

THE FACES OF LOVE

Let's revisit Paul's revelation of the love of God one more time. He wrote, "and that you, being rooted and grounded in love, may be able to comprehend with all the saints what is the *breadth and length and height and depth*, and to know the love of Christ which surpasses knowledge" (Ephesians 3:17–19, emphasis added).

The love of Jesus is multidimensional; it has *breadth*. It is an extensive, all-encompassing ocean of adoration that surrounds you with compassion and woos you with admiration. It covers you in dark seasons and protects you through the night. It greets you in the morning and smiles on you through the day. It is captured at dusk and expressed at dawn. It is hope to the discouraged and peace to the lost.

The love of Jesus has *length*; it goes the distance. You can't fall so far that it can't catch you, run so fast that it can't get you, or hide so well that it can't find you. His love is better than your worst day, stronger than the most defiant will, and more forgiving than your cruelest sin. When you give up, love goes on; when you fall down, it picks you up. Love is courage to the fearful, hope to the helpless, strength to the weary, and wealth to the impoverished. Love goes the distance!

The agape love of Christ has *height*; it exceeds all your expectations. Paul emphasizes this dimension of God's love in the next verse when he writes that God "is able to do exceedingly abundantly above all that we ask or think, according to the power that works in us" (Ephesians 3:20 NKJV). If you asked for it, love gives more; if you thought it, love takes it higher. If you dream big, love dreams bigger; if you aim high, love aims higher. You dream of a family; love dreams of a legacy. You ask for a job; love finds you a destiny. You hope for peace; love longs for a ministry. You pray for heaven; love gives you His city. Go ahead, think really big . . . but it will never compare to what love has already planned for you!

God's love has *depth*; it is intense, complex, profound, and able to penetrate your soul. Love's revelation perpetually unfolds as you peer into its substance and experience its splendor. Love is like poetry that awakens the mind to colors so vivid and beauty divine. Like an ocean so deep or a universe so vast, it beckons to be discovered and longs to be grasped. Mysteries and wonders unfold at your feet, and as you walk with His love, your fears He defeats. Deeper and deeper you tumble into God, enriched by His goodness and changed by His love. The depth of this mystery is hard to explain, for the ocean that is around you is in you, just the same.

LOVE WORKING IN YOU

Jesus said, "You shall love your neighbor as yourself" (Matthew 22:39). Did you catch the word *as*? It's profound how two small letters can change everything in your life. The word *as* means, "equally, since, when, like, because, or in the same way." Let's try a couple of these synonyms in the sentence, and see what emerges.

"Love your neighbor *since* you love yourself." How about this one: "Love your neighbor *because* you love yourself." In other words, you loving you is the foundation for you loving them: the people around you, your neighbor, your enemies, your family, and your God!

Many people let the love of God work *through* them, but they refuse to let God's love work *in* them. I often hear people quote scriptures out of context to validate their lack of self-respect and self-love. For example, how many times have you heard this one: "I am just a sinner saved by grace." Doesn't this sound so humble? Actually, it points to an issue of pride.

The difference between humility and pride is that humility acknowledges the source of greatness as God. Therefore, it is Christ-centered. Humility isn't thinking less of yourself; it's thinking of yourself less. On the other hand, pride is self-made, ungrateful, entitled, and self-centered. Consider this: thinking badly about yourself is still prideful, because you made yourself the center of attention again . . . it's still all about you.

> HUMILITY ISN'T THINKING LESS OF YOURSELF; IT'S THINKING OF YOURSELF LESS.

Let me clear the fog hiding who you truly are because of God's love. You were a sinner before you knew Jesus, but as soon as you received Him into your heart you became a saint! The apostle Paul wrote, "God demonstrates His own love toward us, in that while we were yet sinners, Christ died for us" (Romans 5:8). Christ gave His life for you when you were still prone to evil and an enemy of God. But then Jesus delivered you from darkness and purged the darkness from you. Suddenly you became the light of the world, and the righteousness of God in Christ Jesus.

Now you are a new creation; those old, evil things are gone from your soul. You are royalty, nobility, a holy nation, and sons and daughters of the King Himself. You are joint heirs with Christ, you carry His divine nature, and you have His mind so you think as God does. You are currently seated with Jesus on the same throne (it must be a big seat) in heavenly places.

When you say you're a sinner, you are telling Jesus, "What You did on the cross was enough to save me, but it wasn't enough to transform me." That's stupid, and stupid is painful! Stupid can keep you from loving yourself, and if you don't love yourself you can't love anyone else! So do the world a favor, and begin to embrace God's love for you by reminding yourself that you were born to be amazing because you were modeled after your Maker.

Love That Redefines You

My own struggle with low God-esteem (my perspective of God's view of me) is well documented in my first book, *The Supernatural Ways of Royalty*. I have a PhD in self-hatred and self-condemnation. I spent the first forty years of my life building cases against other people, because I had a log stuck in my heart's eye. I have come a long way in the last several years, yet the stench of low self-esteem still rears its ugly head at times.

The other day I had an incredible experience. Kathy and I were doing a photo shoot for our new blog. I hate people taking pictures of me, so I was not looking forward to the evening.

The Bethel media team arrived at my house with strawberries and M&Ms, my favorite junk food. A great beginning! Before they began taking pictures they all commented on how amazing we looked, how beautiful we were, and how great the pictures were going to turn out. I was thinking, *Yeah, yeah, yeah, whatever!*

As they shot each picture they looked into the tiny screen on the camera and said, "Wow, that looks amazing." "Well, that's beautiful!" "Now that's a great picture . . . you two are so photogenic." "That's a really great pose. You look great in that picture!" I kept thinking, *Are you taking pictures of me? What the heck are you seeing in that little screen?*

After about fifty shots, they said, "Let's show you a few of the pictures." As they flipped from screen to screen on the small camera viewer, they kept saying, "Isn't that a beautiful picture? Wow! You look great in that picture. That shirt looks awesome on you. You and Kathy are so beautiful together! You guys look like models!"

I thought I looked fat, tired, and old; but as they continued to describe what *they* saw in the pictures, a new self-image began to form in my mind. I started to see the photographs from their perspectives. I have to say that was one of the most amazing experiences of my life.

After the team left, Kathy and I sat on the couch together trying to describe what had just happened. There is something special about being in the presence of people who think you're beautiful. It has a way of reforming you, reminding you, transforming the way you think about yourself. It's love in action. It's nourishment for your soul. Love is the inner health you need in order to walk freely in the purposes of God for your life.

I have a dream that each of us would create a culture that cultivates world-changers by loving unconditionally. Our love would be so incredibly deep that people would feel enveloped with a deep sense of belonging, and they would lose the fear of failure. I think *The Message* captures the essence of what I envision when it describes love:

> Love never gives up.
> Love cares more for others than for self.
> Love doesn't want what it doesn't have.
> Love doesn't strut,
> Doesn't have a swelled head,
> Doesn't force itself on others,
> Isn't always "me first,"
> Doesn't fly off the handle,
> Doesn't keep score of the sins of others,
> Doesn't revel when others grovel,
> Takes pleasure in the flowering of truth,
> Puts up with anything,
> Trusts God always,
> Always looks for the best,
> Never looks back,
> But keeps going to the end.
>
> (1 CORINTHIANS 13:4–7)

This is the kind of love that transforms people! This covenant love causes people to be fully actualized, because they know they are loved beyond their ability to perform.

For example, when coaches demonstrate this kind of love, their players know they are more important than the game. This gives them confidence to live out loud on the court, field, track, or pool. Conversely, when players are loved conditionally and shouted at continually for their mistakes, fear begins to seep into their souls. This ultimately undermines their ability to think clearly. They begin second-guessing every move they make and, consequently, they lose the capacity to act from instinct and muscle memory.

The ability to play from instinct and muscle memory is the catalyst that triggers what is often described as the "zone" in the sports world. Many athletes describe the zone as a kind of mystical experience where the game suddenly switches to slow motion, giving them the ability to anticipate the trajectory of the ball and act accordingly. Basketball players add another element to the zone. They say the zone causes the basket to double in size, which leads to their shot percentage skyrocketing.

Of course, my sports illustration is just an example of what happens when people are immersed in a culture that accepts them for who they are and refuses to punish them when they fail. Catalytic cultures that cultivate greatness speak more often to people's potential than to their problems.

If you want to reach your full potential in God, you will need to find a culture where love flows through you, to you, and around you, or create one. Anything less will reduce your capacity, or at least delay your destiny.

The Weak Things
Confound the Wise

In 2012 I, along with several friends, visited Winston Churchill's home. It's a large rustic mansion, with hand-hewn beams and plank floors. The trophies that fill the cabinets in many of the rooms impressed a lot of the tourists. But I was drawn to the worn places where Churchill must have walked and knelt often. A discolored leather chair captured my attention in a room where Winston sat a lot. I imagined him there during those tough war-torn days, contemplating and praying for wisdom or pacing the floor in deep thought. A well-used desk stood proudly in a den where Churchill crafted many of his speeches. I was overwhelmed by the sense of nobility that filled the room. I loved that the home felt lived in . . . imperfect, marred, scarred, and worn. There was an intrinsic beauty about the old mansion: walls that told stories, floors that whispered secrets, furniture that hinted at mysteries.

I sat on a bench outside Churchill's front door for a long time reflecting on the revelation that was seeping into my soul by simply being in the same space once occupied by a broken but great man.

I thought about how I liked things perfect, shiny, and flawless; but at the end of the day, most things that are perfect are also lifeless, mechanical, plastic replicas of the real thing. Somehow the beauty of humanity lies in its flaws, frailties, and weaknesses, like worn patterns in wood floors that reveal pathways and passions, marks on thresholds made by those who toiled there. At the end of the day, it's the real and the rustic (not the robotic, programmed, and predictable) that give us a sense of what is truly beautiful.

PhDs Are Not for Me

Recently, a friend of mine, the chancellor of a Christian university in the United States, called and offered me an earned doctorate from his university. I have no formal education beyond high school, so I was very interested. I think he offered me the degree mainly because his university uses several of my books in its ministry track, which I helped to develop.

The plan was for me to write a dissertation and challenge all the subjects that made up the ministry track. I was very excited about the opportunity to earn my doctorate—and in less than a year. To make matters better, the university agreed to use the manuscript I had written about empowering women, which I had just completed, as my dissertation. All I had to do was reformat it.

I called my mother to give her the good news. She wept on the phone and told me how proud she was of me. Several months passed, and things progressed quickly with the help of my personal assistant, Beth, who reformatted my entire manuscript to meet the requirements of my dissertation.

Then one night I woke up out of a dead sleep, and I heard the Lord ask me a question: "You never talked to me about getting a PhD at a university. What do you think you're doing?"

"Lord, I am kind of excited about getting my degree. You know I have no education to speak of, so this will give me a lot of credibility with people," I responded.

"Kris, if you have letters after your name, people will think you can be great on your own, and we both know that you can't! You were born to be an example of what I can do with weakness. When people observe your life and see who you have become and what you have accomplished in the midst of your faults, failures, flaws, frailties, and weaknesses, they will know that your greatness is rooted in Me. Your life was meant to be an inspiration for the weak and the broken. Many people will put their trust in Me because of what I do through you. Now call the university, and cancel your doctorate!"

I cried the rest of the night. I didn't realize how deeply rooted my desire was to be admired by people who were highly educated and intelligent. But I knew the Lord was right.

The fact is, I've written eleven books, four manuals, and developed five curricula to date, and I absolutely can't spell! To make matters worse, I can barely type. When I was writing my first book, *The Supernatural Ways of Royalty*, I didn't understand how spell-check worked on Microsoft Word.

One day I was working on my manuscript, "typing" away at a brisk pace, when my wife, Kathy, quietly came up behind me. Unbeknownst to me, she was watching me "type" my manuscript. Suddenly a box appeared on the screen, as it did every few seconds, which read, "No spelling suggestions. Do you want to add this to your dictionary?" I checked yes.

"Did you just check 'yes' on the word processor?" she questioned.

"Yeah, what's the problem?"

She burst out laughing! "Do you have any idea what you are doing?"

"Well, I thought I did, but now I'm thinking maybe I don't."

Several minutes passed as Kathy tried to stop laughing long enough to explain to me that my word processor now spoke in tongues with no interpretation!

Nine years have passed since I wrote my first book, and in my defense, I have learned quite a bit about writing. But I still can't spell, nor do I type very well. Yet something phenomenal happens to me every time I sit down to write; I see concepts and pictures in my mind. Then I often hear this inner voice that tells me to paint with words. At the risk of being misunderstood or being thought of as hyperspiritual, I have to say that the Holy Spirit actually taught (and is still teaching) me to write!

To be clear, I'm not stupid, but I am flawed and weak in certain areas. The difficulty is that the places where my flaws and weaknesses show up the most are in the areas I am called to. I guess this is sort of obvious. I mean, if you can't sing, and you don't sing, then your weaknesses are covered in that you stay away from the stuff you're not good at. But if you can't type, and you can't spell, yet you are called to be an author, then you are working in your weakness, not ministering in your strength. And though it might not make sense according to worldly logic, somehow it does in light of God. The great apostle Paul put it best: "[The Lord] has said to me, 'My grace is sufficient for you, for power is perfected in weakness.' Most gladly, therefore, I will rather boast about my weaknesses, so that the power of Christ may dwell in me. Therefore I am well content with weaknesses . . . for Christ's sake; for when I am weak, then I am strong" (2 Corinthians 12:9–11).

I'm certainly not promoting a doctrine of ignorance or a policy of anti-education. I would never go to a medical doctor who was "taught by the Holy Spirit" and hadn't graduated from medical school. So, please, if you are called to a vocation that requires higher education, get a degree and pursue it with all your heart, and with all of your mind, and with all of your strength.

> IT'S IN OUR FLAWS AND WEAKNESSES THAT THE INTRINSIC BEAUTY OF OUR CREATOR SHINES THROUGH OUR BROKENNESS: LIGHT REFRACTING THROUGH HUMANITY MANIFESTING IN THE MANY COLORS OF HIS NATURE.

What I am saying is that you need to do the world a favor and be an original! We have enough cubic zirconia Christians . . . manmade, perfect imitations. The world is hungry for diamonds whose beauty was created from the pressures of life (not images manufactured by some marketing campaign). The awe of believers with all of their flaws exposed under the microscope of public inspection is indeed attractive. It's in our flaws and weaknesses that the intrinsic beauty of our Creator shines through our brokenness: light refracting through humanity manifesting in the many colors of His nature. When and where we are weak, He is strong, and His strength is revealed by our weaknesses.

Hiding Your Weaknesses

In Western culture there is a lot of pressure to hide our weaknesses and flaws. The older we get, the more aware we become that youth and beauty are in vogue, while age and weakness are unpopular. So in a desperate attempt to be valued, we hide our vulnerabilities and disguise our frailties. We dye our gray hair, have face-lifts, and try our best to ward off any sign of imperfection. Yet, for most of us, this only delays the inevitable.

According to Brené Brown, a social researcher with a PhD and three degrees in social work, there are some extremely destructive side effects to hiding our weaknesses. When Brené set out to discover the root cause of society's core constraints and dysfunctions, she found, unsurprisingly, that the greatest need of the human heart is the desire to feel connected, loved, and known. But what she uncovered next was astounding.[1]

Shame is at the root of society's brokenness.

Brené defines *shame* as "the fear of disconnection." Interestingly, the fear of disconnection ("I am afraid you are not going to like me") is also the main cause of disconnection. In other words, shame is the archenemy of connection.

There's a difference between guilt and shame. Guilt says, "You did something wrong," while shame says, "You are something wrong! You are not good enough, smart enough, pretty enough, experienced enough, spiritual enough, and so forth, to be loved and accepted." Needless to say, shame robs you of your sense of approval.

As Brené dug deeper into shame, she found that people who live in shame have deep feelings of unworthiness. In other words, the reason shame has such a strong hold on their hearts is that they don't think they deserve to be loved. Of course this causes them to hide in order to protect their hearts, but hiding only helps create the ecosystem of disconnection.

Let me explain how it works: you feel unworthy, therefore you feel ashamed. You are ashamed, so you hide. And when you hide, you feel disconnected. When you are disconnected, you feel unworthy . . . and the beat goes on!

The most common way to cope with this unhealthy cycle is to numb the pain, so often people medicate shame with drugs, drown it in pornography, satisfy it by binge eating, or blame their pain on others. Of course, none of this ever really works.

To make matters worse, you can't selectively numb your pain; therefore, when you numb your pain you also numb yourself to joy, pleasure, excitement, and so on. Thus life becomes drudgery, a place where you survive but never thrive.

So what's the answer? Brené discovered that *vulnerability* is what breaks the cycle of shame and disconnection. You read that right; being "real" extinguishes the fires of shame and eliminates the ash heap of disconnection.

What does it mean to be vulnerable? It's saying "I love you" first, risking rejection, and being transparent. Vulnerability is being seen, being known, and being real. It is coming to terms with our weaknesses and embracing them as gifts from God! Paul put it this way: "God hath chosen the foolish things of the world to confound the wise; and God hath chosen the weak things of the world to confound the things which are mighty" (1 Corinthians 1:27 KJV).

The wounds of a warrior are actually badges of honor that should be celebrated, not covered up. To the young, the untrained, and the inexperienced, vulnerabilities may seem to be ugly flaws—disqualifying marks of life's failures—or proof of the irrelevance of those who are aging, hidden away in homes, or forced into obscurity.

Yet God often hides his greatest treasures in the weak, in those who are scarred or can no longer perform. For most people, such treasures remain buried and forgotten, marked by stones and visited with flowers on special occasions. (Sometimes it's easier to pay respects to the dead than it is to value the living.)

But it is the wise and discerning who view weakness through the eyes of the Kingdom and choose to connect often with and receive impartations from those the world considers weak. Like Jacob, who received an inheritance from his elderly blind father when Isaac laid hands on his younger son and transformed his life forever, we have a divine opportunity for impartation and connection. But first we must change our value systems so we can perceive God's treasures for what they are.

Heaven Waits for Real

Our heavenly Father's high value for weakness and authenticity is beautifully expressed in the meeting that Jesus had with the woman at the well. You probably know the story told in John 4:7–38. Jesus asked the Samaritan woman to give him a drink from the well. She was pretty shocked for two reasons: it was illegal for a man to talk to a woman in public, and she was a Samaritan! Jews saw the Samaritans as sinful, shameful half-breeds: they had the same Israelite heritage as the Jews, but their theology and culture had been corrupted by centuries of foreign conquest and occupation. So, of course, she resisted giving Jesus a drink.

> Therefore the Samaritan woman said to Him, "How is it that You, being a Jew, ask me for a drink since I am a Samaritan woman?" (For Jews have no dealings with Samaritans.)
>
> Jesus answered and said to her, "If you knew the gift of God, and who it is who says to you, 'Give me a drink,' you would have asked Him, and He would have given you living water" (John 4:9–10)

The Samaritan woman decided to follow suit and give up her prejudice. She said, "You are not greater than our father Jacob, are You, who gave us the well, and drank of it himself and his sons and his cattle?" (4:12).

Did you catch the fact that she acknowledged that Jacob was "our father"? In other words, she was saying, "Jacob is your father and my father, and he gave us both this well." The lady was jumping into the deep end of the relational pool with Jesus.

Within minutes the Samaritan woman realized she was speaking to a holy man, although she was not sure who He was. I suppose by then she was quite nervous, as many men apparently had abused her. She blurted out, "Sir, give me this water, so I will not be thirsty nor come all the way here to draw" (4:16).

Jesus understood the power of vulnerability, so He gave her

an opportunity to be transparent by telling her to bring her husband to Him. Risking ridicule, she responded,

> "I have no husband."
>
> Jesus said to her, "You have correctly said, 'I have no husband'; for you have had five husbands, and the one whom you now have is not your husband; this you have said truly" (4:17–18).

I've heard many people say that Jesus was exposing her sin. That's not true! Jesus was connecting with her brokenness and inviting her out of shame. You see, in those days wives could not divorce their husbands; only husbands could divorce their wives. Therefore, this woman had been rejected five times, thrown away like a piece of trash. To make matters worse, the man she was with at that moment wouldn't even marry her. Jesus didn't say she was an adulterer. Instead He said, "I know your hurt, your pain, your shame, and your brokenness, and I love you anyway."

The Samaritan woman's response was not one of conviction but of connection. Her shame of rejection quickly evaporated in the transparency of vulnerability. Think about it. Jesus spoke to her; He transcended the cultural confines of prejudice and gave her value. He asked her to give Him a drink. He became vulnerable by exposing His own need to her, and then He asked her to meet it. Then He invited the Samaritan woman to ask Him for a drink of living water. He made it clear that He valued her in spite of the brokenness He perceived in her.

She struggled to comprehend her encounter, but Jesus was a safe place for her to be real. She decided to be honest and let Jesus know that she questioned her own faith. She went on to ask Him to teach her about God's desire for worship. She said to Him, "Sir, I perceive that You are a prophet. Our fathers worshiped in this mountain, and you people say that in Jerusalem is the place where men ought to worship" (John 4:19–20).

Instead of just answering her theological question, Jesus used the opportunity to lead her out of shame and into wholeness. He said to her, "Woman, believe Me, an hour is coming when neither in this mountain nor in Jerusalem will you worship the Father . . . but an hour is coming, and now is, when the true worshipers will worship the Father in spirit and truth; for such people the Father seeks to be His worshipers" (4:21, 23).

Jesus made it clear to her that the Father is looking for worshipers who are not defined by their ethnic origins (Jews or Samaritans), but are spiritual truth tellers. The Greek word for *truth* in this context means "nothing hidden; real and authentic." Jesus was inviting this woman, with all of her rejection, brokenness, and abandonment issues, to be a worshiper, to come close to the Father and be made whole.

Shameless in Paradise

Okay, let's pull this all together. The core reasons we were created and put on this planet were for connections and relationships with God and one another. The enemy of connection is shame, but the cure for shame is vulnerability, the ability to be fully known. Vulnerability is facilitated through authenticity. Authenticity means letting go of who others want you to be, so you can be who you really are. These are the kind of worshipers heaven is looking for: those who are shameless and unafraid of their weaknesses, who know the beauty that God works into their brokenness because they live in the light where there is nothing hidden. In other words, what you see is what you get!

Jesus is the Master of inviting people out of their caves of shame and into the light of His countenance. David said, "In Your light we see light" (Psalm 36:9). As Jesus did with the Samaritan woman, He sheds light on your divine identity when He draws near to you.

What happens when Jesus sets you free from shame and invites you into the holy circle of worshipers? I'll tell you what happens: you go get all your friends and invite them to come and meet Him. That's exactly what happened with the Samaritan woman! She went back to her city and told everyone about her encounter with Jesus. His love for one broken woman was so moving that the whole city turned out to meet Him. This is the power of vulnerability, transparency, and loving connection.

My concern today is that people are increasingly leading virtual lives that keep them in hiding. They go to the gym to work out on the treadmill where they run but go nowhere. They watch themselves run on a virtual trail, but in reality they haven't moved a foot. Then they go home and watch Bethel TV and think they've gone to church, although they haven't actually had fellowship with anyone. Nobody has personally spoken into their lives because they only have virtual leaders. Later they go to the movies and have a fictional adventure, watching actors live the lives they wish they had the courage to live. They go back home and get on Facebook, Twitter, and Instagram to "connect" with their two hundred remote friends who know them only by their profiles and their photoshopped pictures. Some of them even post terrible comments to "friends" they never had about things they watched on YouTube. Worse yet, many assassinate the characters of people they never knew using courage that never existed.

It's such a tragedy.

The most vulnerable victims of this virtual generation are the kids who are raised by virtual parents. I was a part of the latchkey-kid generation: children raised by babysitters instead of a mom and dad. But now the machines are nurturing our children. That's right! Video games have taken the place of real people! And do you know who wrote the software that is keeping your children company? A generation raised by babysitters! Ironic, isn't it?

We used to watch sci-fi movies about machines taking over the world. Of course, we all thought it was just entertainment at the time. Little did we know that those machines would some-day be training our children. Nowadays most kids know their machines better than they know their folks. They spend so much time learning virtual video skills that many of them don't know how to do real life with human beings. The beauty of the real, the sincere—the result of God working in human weakness—is replaced with loneliness, shame cultivated in hiding, and no true understanding of what it is to press through the difficulties of life. These kids can kill the mutants and rescue the castle, but when it comes time to solve a real conflict with their peers they are clueless.

Why do you think kids are killing their classmates and assassinating their teachers? It just might be because they have exchanged life skills for computer skills. They are ignorant of the things we used to learn in kindergarten—social skills such as share with others, say you're sorry, take turns on the swings, don't hit people, don't make fun of others, have quiet time, and so forth. Machines might be able to teach our kids math and science, but they can't explain to them how to love their neighbors as themselves and how to discover value in each other's imperfections.

Now, let me be clear. I have no problem with video games, social networking, TV, movies, or any of the rest of it—as long as they don't take the place of real life, real relationships, and real love. But people are becoming so disconnected that it's alarming.

I play basketball at the YMCA three times a week. Some of the kids there play the game with their earbuds crammed into their heads and plugged into an iPod. They seem to be afraid of connecting with the people on their ball team. We must correct this! We are raising a generation that lacks people skills. I fear they are going to drown themselves in the sea of isolation.

It's time to rage against the machines. We can beat them—we really can—because love is incalculable, unpredictable, and irresistible. Love never fails, but the machines will become obsolete as powerful humans are enlightened with passion and ignited with purpose!

Let's pull the plugs on the dang machines and live in the reality of vulnerable, shame-free, real relationships.

4

Your Destiny Is in
Your People

The Lone Ranger had a sidekick named Tonto, the great apostle
Paul had Barnabas, Esther had Mordecai, and Ruth had Naomi.
Nobody becomes successful by himself or herself; all of us need
the right people to launch us into our
destiny. It seems as if most of us
are asking what we are called to do
when we should first be asking who
we are supposed to be with. It's only
when we find our people that we can
fulfill our purposes. The truth is,
our purposes lie in our people!

> IT'S ONLY WHEN WE
> FIND OUR PEOPLE
> THAT WE CAN FULFILL
> OUR PURPOSES.

For me, it all began in 1978 when we were living a big-city, fast-paced lifestyle. I was a mess. I'd had a nervous breakdown that resulted in forty to fifty panic attacks a day. I could hardly function, although I never missed a day of work. We moved from the San Francisco Bay Area to Lewiston, California (a tiny community of nine hundred people nestled in the Trinity Alps), so I could heal.

We had our first child the same year, which of course was wonderful, but I was scarcely ready for the added pressure of a child. Kathy and I had both left great jobs to relocate. I was working at an automotive repair shop in Weaverville, another small town of about three thousand people, and after buying our "little house on the prairie," we were completely broke. In fact, we got up early most mornings before work and went fishing down the road from our house so we would have something good to eat for dinner. Times were tough, to say the least. To make matters worse, our spiritual lives were in shambles.

We were going to a little Assemblies of God church with a congregation of about forty people. The people were friendly, but their pastor had left and the elders were trying hard to keep the fellowship from becoming a sinking ship. Little did I know that my life was about to be radically altered forever.

It was Sunday morning, and there was a huge amount of expectation in the air. We walked into the church just in time for our elders to introduce our new pastor and his wife. He certainly didn't look like a pastor to me. He looked like a long-haired hippie, and his wife reminded me of a flower child straight out of Haight-Ashbury. I was saved in the Jesus Movement, so I was accustomed to hanging out with hippies, but I needed a father in my life, not a hipster.

We sang a few boring hymns, and then it was finally time for the hippie pastor to speak. He seemed pretty laid back; he spoke softly, almost peacefully, to the church. By now I had grown used to the Pentecostal hype that would magically overcome anyone who stood behind the podium of our little Podunk chapel. But evidently he didn't get the memo. He seemed to have been inoculated from the customary Pentecostal power play that was sort of the "mark of a different beast" in our church.

Then suddenly something happened, something I was not ready for at all. He asked us to open to a passage of scripture that he subsequently had us read out loud together. Then he began to teach. I had never heard anyone utter words like that in my entire life. He spoke out of the Bible as if he'd had a conversation with God about what he was supposed to share with us. I was stunned; I could hardly get my jaw off the floor. Tears ran down both my cheeks. I honestly didn't know why I was crying, except it felt as if I was drinking ice-cold water in the midst of a hot, dusty desert. Every word was like an oracle from God that pierced my heart and answered the cry of my soul . . . a cry I didn't even know was in me.

When he finished speaking, we all just sat there like a bunch of zombies, not knowing how to respond or what to do. Our hearts longed to say something, but our heads couldn't muster a logical reply. Week after week our hippie-looking pastor continued teaching us like an angel bringing secret messages from some lost heavenly treasure chest.

Time passed, and the weeks quickly turned into months. I fearfully reached out to our pastor, terrified that he would find out how messed up I was and wouldn't reach back to me. But my fears were unwarranted. Not only did he reach back to me, but he took a liking to Kathy and me and soon our families were spending five days a week together. We were practically inseparable for the next twelve years. In fact, we even lived together for six months while we were building our new home.

You may have figured out by now that my hippie pastors were Bill and his wife Beni Johnson. Of course, they weren't really hippies. They were just radical Jesus people, and they still are.

People Change

I had never connected with another person like Bill before. Our relationship wasn't weird in any way; it was inspiring, encouraging, exciting, and exhilarating. I was learning so much about Jesus from Bill's teaching. Yet the most amazing experience I had was just watching Bill love God! It was like a young married couple watching a romantic movie and falling in love again after every scene. Although I didn't understand it at the time, somehow Bill's relationship with God was a catalyst to me being fully actualized.

It seemed as if every day something new was growing inside me—something I didn't even know was there, something I never desired before, something wonderful, something beautiful. In a way that is hard to explain, Jesus was forming in me, and I was coming alive inside.

The real Kris was being watered, cultivated, and celebrated. For the first time in my life I was being invited to be myself. I began to understand that I had spent much of my life trying to be what others needed (or wanted) me to be. I needed so badly to be accepted by my peers that it was too risky to try and discover who I really was. But meeting Bill changed all of that, because a father chose to love me unconditionally. His love and acceptance created a place for me to play the game of life with passion.

All I ever wanted to do in life was love God, raise my family, and build a great automotive business. But some of my desires changed after I met Bill. Suddenly I had an insatiable yearning to lead people into a deeper relationship with God and to teach them all the things we were learning about living successfully in the Kingdom. I was changing so quickly inside that I hardly knew myself.

Many years passed, and in 1996, after seventeen years in Weaverville, Bill and Beni moved to Redding, California, to become the senior leaders of Bethel Church. We didn't see each other much the first year, as we were both very busy. Kathy and I had four businesses; plus we were helping Mountain Chapel weather the leadership transition from Bill to Danny Silk. Of course Bill and Beni had their hands full with Bethel as the church had lost a thousand people during their transition.

The next year I joined Bill on a weeklong ministry trip to my daughter and son-in-law's Youth with a Mission (YWAM) base in Colorado. We stayed in a small cottage together for five days. The ministry time was great, but something even more powerful (maybe even supernatural) happened in the middle of the night in that tiny bungalow.

I would get up in the middle of the night to go to the restroom, and I'd have to pass by Bill's bed. Although he was sound asleep, I could hear him saying, "Jesus, I love you. You are all I ever need in my life. Jesus, you are amazing! Jesus, thank you for loving me." By the fifth night I was completely wrecked. I was a basket case. Two things happened: first, I became so aware of a longing in me for a deeper relationship with Jesus that I cried myself to sleep the entire week. Second, I grew to understand that I was meant to follow Bill and to serve him in his ministry. I honestly lost my desire to pursue anything else.

At the end of the week we flew back to California and had a three-hour layover at the San Francisco airport. I hadn't said a word to Bill about my night experiences or my inner longings. Heck, I wasn't completely sure what was happening inside of me, so how could I even begin to try to express it to someone else, much less Bill? And what if he felt differently? What if the longing was one-sided? I was spinning inside!

To complicate matters, I had not talked to Kathy in a week. What if she thought I was crazy? I knew the first thing she would ask: "How could we leave our businesses, and what about our home we built in the woods that our kids grew up in?" Yikes! I had no answers, none at all!

Bill and I sat across from one another at a table in the airport making small talk. I could tell that Bill was contemplating something by the distant look on his face. A half hour passed, and then he suddenly looked up at me and said, "I want to start a ministry school at Bethel Church, and I really think you and Kathy should oversee the school."

As usual, Bill was calm, while I was trying hard not to look shocked or do something crazy like jump up on a table and shout, "Hallelujah!"

"That would be an honor," I replied, trying to match his

understated demeanor. "I will have to talk to Kathy, and we will pray for God's direction."

I could hardly contain myself as questions began to flood my mind. I tried to calm my gut by reminding myself that this was a long shot that made no practical sense, but nothing I did seemed to work.

By the time I got home to our mountain chalet I was ready to explode. Kathy greeted me at the front door with a kiss, but I wasn't thinking about romance. Before the door could even close behind me, I started giving Kathy a blow-by-blow account of my week. Her excitement grew as I recounted the story, but little did she know that I was about to drop a bomb on her!

I decided to give her the news in small bites.

"Bill would like us to help him start a ministry school in Redding," I said nonchalantly. (I conveniently left out the part about leaving all our worldly possessions behind to do this.)

Several minutes passed as Kathy pelted me with questions. The tension increased exponentially with each of my replies. I could see her assembling the pieces of the puzzle in her mind as I answered each question.

Then her facial expression abruptly changed. "Are you saying that we should leave our businesses, leave our home, and move to Redding?" Before I could respond she continued. "Are you trying to tell me that you want to give up everything we have worked for to follow Bill?"

Before the year was over our businesses were gone, and we were on staff at Bethel Church. God miraculously spoke to Kathy personally and confirmed our call to be with Bill and Beni.

Guided by Dreams

We started the ministry school with thirty-seven full-time students. The early days were wonderful and yet incredibly hard! It was the best and worst of times.

I was having a very hard time working for Bill. The truth was, I had worked for myself for twenty years, and I just didn't like answering to anybody. Bill tried his best to be gracious to me, but nothing he did seemed to solve my problem.

By the third year, I was ready to quit. Through a series of circumstances, I learned that a church about three hours from us was considering asking me to be their senior pastor. I was excited to have an exit plan. But when I explained the plan to Bill, he seemed genuinely sorry I was considering leaving. I was taken aback by his response, as I thought that he would be just as excited to see me leave as I was to go.

In the midst of this process I had a vivid dream. In the dream I was preaching in my new church, and the place was packed to the walls. There was even a sound system set up in the parking lot, and about a thousand people were listening to me preach outside. Then God said to me, "This is what will happen if you leave Bethel and become the pastor of this church." I was stunned! But the scene in the dream changed. Now I was looking at the earth from outer space through something like the Hubble telescope. I heard God say, "If you leave Bill, you will never impact the earth! It's your choice." He continued, "If you decide to leave, only you and I will know you failed. It will be our secret!"

Yikes, I thought, *Leaving doesn't seem like an option!*

I was troubled after that dream because I had my heart set

on leaving. To make matters worse, Bill and I still weren't getting along, yet I knew this was a word from the Lord. A few months passed before I finally got the courage to ask God what I should do. Immediately I heard Him say, "Make a covenant with Bill to serve with him the rest of your life!"

A couple months passed as I wrestled with God over this issue. The Lord was kind to me but relentless. He kept reminding me of those nights in that cabin, how I longed for connection, how I knew we were destined to be together.

I finally got off the wrestling mat with the Lord and decided to do the right thing no matter the cost. I waited until Bill and I were by ourselves for five hours driving to a retreat. I mustered up the courage to share my vision. With tears running down my face I said, "I want to make a covenant with you to serve alongside you the rest of my life." It was nighttime, so the darkness hid my tears from him.

"Great!" he responded (obviously not understanding the depth of my agony). That was it. There was no lightning or thunder, no audible voice from heaven shouting, "This is My beloved son in whom I am well pleased," no angels singing, nothing. Just, "Great!"

About a month later Bill expressed his own lifetime commitment to Kathy and me. I realize now that Bill believed we were already in covenant together for life, and that's why he was so surprised when I unveiled my plans to leave. I was the one who needed to express my commitment to him so that my heart had no other options. Thankfully it wasn't long after this that my heart completely turned around.

I began to understand that God had created Bill and me to serve together. There was never any doubt we needed each other.

Our gifts were so different and complementary, but it was more than that. We were members of His body, and we fit together perfectly. It was as if the right hand divinely found and fused itself to the right arm.

> WE ARE CALLED TO INFLUENCE THE WORLD, AND YOU CAN'T DO THAT BY YOURSELF!

Since that day our ministries have grown exponentially, as God has graciously granted us influence with both the poor and the powerful of the world. Separately, we could have done some good ministry, but we are called to influence the world, and you can't do that by yourself!

Who Is with You?

Everywhere I go people seem obsessed with finding their destiny. The million-dollar question appears to be, "Why am I alive, and what was I born to do?"

The New Age Movement is feeding off this intense fascination people have with their purpose. Psychic hotlines are buzzing with people looking for insight into their futures. Even books such as *The Purpose Driven Life*, authored by Rick Warren, have sold millions of copies as people wrestle with God's intent for their lives. I taught people for years that next to finding God, the most important thing they can do in life is find their purposes. But I was wrong! Let me explain.

I do believe that discovering your destiny is extremely important. Paul put it this way: "I have fought the good fight, I have finished the course, I have kept the faith; in the future there is laid up for me the crown of righteousness, which the Lord, the righteous Judge, will award to me on that day . . ." (2 Timothy 4:7–8).

It's true that we each have a race to run and a fight to finish. God has given each of us a specific assignment to complete in our lifetimes. Paul also wrote, "we are His workmanship, created in Christ Jesus for *good works*, which God prepared beforehand so that we would walk in them" (Ephesians 2:10, emphasis added). Yes, it is true that each of us has a purpose and a destiny in God.

But you can't find your purpose until you have found your people, because your ultimate purpose is in your people! People ask me all the time if I had a vision for ministry when I was a boy. No! My vision grew out of the role I played with the people I was called to be in community with.

We are the body of Christ. If I am a finger, I need to connect with a hand. If I am an eye, I need to find my place in the head, and so forth. I simply can't find my ultimate destiny without finding my God-given place in the body.

The biblical story of Ruth is a beautiful example of the point I am trying to make. The story opens with an Israelite man named Elimelech, his wife Naomi, and their two sons Mahlon and Chilion moving to the land of Moab to escape a famine in Judah.

Elimelech died soon after they arrived in Moab. Then Mahlon and Chilion married two Moabite women named Orpah and Ruth. Ten years passed, and Mahlon and Chilion both died, leaving Naomi alone with her two daughters-in-law and no grandchildren.

Naomi was old, and she had no choice but to return to Judah and find extended family members who might care for her. Her daughters-in-law needed to do the same thing, but their families were in Moab. This is where the story gets really interesting.

Naomi said to her two daughters-in-law, "Go, return each of you to her mother's house. May the LORD deal kindly with you as you have dealt with the dead and with me. May the LORD grant that you may find rest, each in the house of her husband." Then she kissed them, and they lifted up their voices and wept. . . . Naomi said, "Return, my daughters. Why should you go with me? Have I yet sons in my womb, that they may be your husbands? Return, my daughters!" . . . And they lifted up their voices and wept again; and Orpah kissed her mother-in-law [and went back to the land of Moab], but Ruth clung to her.

Then [Naomi] said [to Ruth], "Behold, your sister-in-law has gone back to her people and her gods; return after your sister-in-law." But Ruth said, "Do not urge me to leave you or turn back from following you; for where you go, I will go, and where you lodge, I will lodge. Your people shall be my people, and your God, my God. Where you die, I will die, and there I will be buried. Thus may the LORD do to me, and worse, if anything but death parts you and me." When she saw that she was determined to go with her, she said no more to her (Ruth 1:8–9, 11–12, 14–18).

Unlike most people in our day who are out for themselves, Ruth refused to follow Near Eastern practices that would have dictated her destiny; instead, she insisted on staying with Naomi. She had found her people, and she knew it!

Think about it. Naomi had nothing to give Ruth: she had no money, no platform, no fame, no fanfare, no future. She was just a poor, old woman! Yet Ruth didn't care because she was not looking for riches or fame. Ruth understood the power of covenant when she said, "May death be the only thing that separates us!"

Even though some couples repeat Ruth's declaration in their marriage vows, they often still live as "friends with benefits." This generation has exchanged the power of covenant for the instant gratification of cohabitation. Consequently, they try to get from lust what can only come from true love.

A cohabitating relationship says, "I'm in this relationship for what I can get from you. Therefore, I am only in this relationship as long as you please me." People who live together without being married often excuse themselves by saying marriage is just a piece of paper. I say, "If it's just a piece of paper, then why don't you sign it?" The truth is, they don't sign it because they use the fear of abandonment to manipulate each other to get what they want! The cohabitating couple doesn't want to make an agreement that lasts forever, because that will take away the element of insecurity they use to keep their partner under pressure to perform.

Those who cohabit find it very difficult to commit to someone forever because they have very little control over how their partners will treat them in the future. Yet in a covenant relationship, it is easier to make a lifetime commitment because the couple is in it for what they can give to the relationship, and they have complete control over their own behaviors.

I call the cohabitating mind-set the "Judas spirit." Let me explain why. Jesus had twelve apostles, and at the Last Supper He basically said to them, "Let's make a covenant." He took bread and said, "This is My body that is broken for you, and this wine is the blood of the new covenant I make with you." As soon as Judas realized that covenant was required, his cover was blown (see Luke 22:19–22).

Judas was a false apostle. He betrayed Jesus with a kiss because he wanted intimacy without covenant (Luke 22:47). He was in relationship with Jesus for what he could get out of it. When he realized that Jesus was about to require Judas to sacrifice himself, he sold out what was left of his stock in Christ for thirty pieces of silver. He didn't want to be in a relationship that cost him.

Judas and Orpah, Naomi's other daughter-in-law, share an interesting connection. In rabbinic literature, known as Midrash, rabbis seeking to fill in the gaps of the Torah posit that Orpah's given name was *Harafa*. The name *Orpah* in Hebrew could mean, "threshed." It was probably given to her after her husband died, because she was "ground like braised corn" as she is believed to have lived a life of promiscuity. Orpah (Harafa) eventually became the mother of four Philistine giants, including Goliath who David killed as recorded in the Bible![1]

Orpah, like Judas, kissed Naomi goodbye. Meanwhile Ruth "clung" to Naomi and made a covenant with her for life. She was not in relationship with Naomi for what she could get; instead she was connected for life, for love, and for God. What happens next is stunning.

Once Ruth and Naomi reached Judah, they had to start over with very little. Ruth began gleaning from the fields to feed both of them. One day a rich and powerful guy named Boaz saw Ruth in his field and inquired about her. He found out that Ruth was a widow. Soon Ruth met Boaz, and he extended kindness to Ruth and Naomi by giving them food and taking care of their needs. A little later, Naomi instructed Ruth to go to Boaz while he slept and lay at his feet. When he woke up she was to ask him to "spread his covering over her," which was a euphemism for the consummation of a marriage. Ruth was asking him to be her kinsman-redeemer.

Boaz was rocked by Ruth. He fell in love with her and married her. Ruth got pregnant and gave birth to a son. They named him Obed. Obed became the father of Jesse, who became the father of King David, who was an ancestor of Jesus!

The prophet Isaiah, speaking of Jesus, prophesied that the throne of David would last into eternity:

> There will be no end to the increase of His government
>> or of peace,
> On the throne of David and over his kingdom,
> To establish it and to uphold it with justice and
>> righteousness
> From then on and forevermore.
> The zeal of the LORD of hosts will accomplish this.
>
> (ISAIAH 9:7)

Okay, let's recap what happened here. Orpah left Naomi and was never mentioned in Scripture again. On the other hand, Ruth clung to Naomi. She refused to chase her own dreams, go after her destiny, or live for herself. Ruth's covenant sacrifice laid

a foundation for her to give birth to Obed, the eventual grandfather of King David. David, a man after God's heart, forged a
legacy that will last into eternity, which includes the Son of God!
It's an understatement to say that finding our people and living in
covenant has eternal consequences.

Changed into Another Man

There are many reasons why it's imperative that we spend our
lives with the right people, but one of the most profound reasons
is hidden in the life of King Saul.

Saul was once a farm boy who didn't know he was called
to be the king of Israel. Through divine providence, when Saul
set out to find his father's lost donkeys one day, he encountered
the prophet Samuel who had already been briefed by God about
Saul's call to be king. Samuel stunned Saul by telling him that
the donkeys he was searching for had already been found. He
went on to insist that Saul stay overnight so that Samuel could
anoint him king in the morning (1 Samuel 9:1–21). It's amazing
that a person can be searching for donkeys one minute and find
his destiny the next.

In the passage, Samuel instructs Saul,

> "You will come to the hill of God where the Philistine garrison
> is; and it shall be as soon as you have come there to the city,
> that you will meet a group of prophets coming down from
> the high place with harp, tambourine, flute, and a lyre before
> them, and they will be prophesying. Then the Spirit of the

LORD will come upon you mightily, and you shall prophesy with them and be changed into another man. . . ."

And when [Saul and Samuel] came to the hill there, behold, a group of prophets met him; and the Spirit of God came upon him mightily, so that he prophesied among them. It came about, when all who knew him previously saw that he prophesied now with the prophets, that the people said to one another, "What has happened to the son of Kish? Is Saul also among the prophets?" A man there said, "Now, who is their father?" Therefore it became a proverb: "Is Saul also among the prophets?" (1 Samuel 10:5–6, 11–12).

Let's review what took place in Saul's life. Saul received a powerful prophecy that he was to be Israel's first king. The next day Saul was anointed and commissioned, but Saul had to meet his people before he could fulfill his purpose. Why, you ask? Because meeting his people changed him into another man . . . the man he needed to be to lead his people.

Saul's life could have been an inspiring story of what happens when you connect with the people God places in your life to reach His purposes for you; but sadly, his success was short-lived. Saul's kingship began strong, and he had several military victories that helped to free the Israelites from the oppression of their enemies. But over time he allowed insecurity, bitterness, and low self-esteem to move back into his heart, which caused him to revert to the man he was before he met the prophets.

Eventually Saul's bitterness opened the door to tormenting demons that drove him mad. He ended up pursuing David for seventeen years in a demonic rage and made several attempts on his life. He killed anyone he thought was helping to protect David.

But then, during one of his worst demonic exploits, Saul encountered the prophets at Ramah and was suddenly changed back into the man he was created to be. Overcome by God, Saul stripped off his clothes and began prophesying with the prophets. The Israelites were shocked by Saul's sudden conversion and began asking one another again, "Is Saul also among the prophets?" (1 Samuel 19:18–24). Unfortunately, the story doesn't end there, because Saul refused to stay connected to his people (the prophets), and ultimately his madness returned.

He later died on the battlefield with his noble son Jonathan, and David became king in his place. Sadly, Saul lacked the character it takes to live an authentic life in a healthy community, and the very things Saul feared came upon him in the end.

Who Are You Hanging Out With?

There is an old adage based on Proverbs 13:20: "Show me your friends, and I will show you your destiny." It's impossible to escape the fact that our destinies lie in our people. Yes, we need God first and foremost, but God also designed us to need one another.

Think about it: would Paul have become an apostle if Barnabas hadn't taken "hold of him" when he was still young in the faith? (Acts 9:27). It's possible that Barnabas inspired Paul to write as many as thirteen books of the Bible. Then later, when Paul refused to take Mark with them on their second missionary journey, Barnabas took hold of Mark and discipled him as well

(Acts 15:36–39). Years later, Mark went on to write the gospel of Mark! Barnabas is not credited with writing books of the Bible, but he mentored two of the most prominent authors of the New Testament.

How about Esther? Do you think Esther would have become a queen without Mordecai? I seriously doubt it! The stories go on and on.

There's Joseph, who met Pharaoh and prepared Egypt to survive a severe famine. There's David, who made a covenant with Jonathan and later became the king of Israel in his father's place. There's Peter, James, and John. In fact, Jesus always sent His disciples out in no less than groups of two. The apostles continued the same pattern in the early days of the church, always sending people out in teams.

The Bible is not alone in its revelation of the communal roots of destiny. In his bestselling book *Good to Great*, author Jim Collins reveals his profound discovery. While nearly everyone was teaching that the most important principle in business was having a vision for an organization, Collins revealed that the organizations that "get the right people on the bus" have the greatest success. He went on to say if you get the right people in the right seats in the bus, inevitably the bus will end up at the right place![2] What Collins uncovered in his research altered the foundation of leadership philosophy in the secular world.

We have found this principle to be accurate at Bethel Church. Over the last twenty years, we have worked hard to choose the right people to be on the Bethel bus. The results have been stunning for both Bethel and for the people on our bus.

For example, Bethel now has more than twenty-two published

authors on staff. Do you know what's most intriguing about this number? Not one of these people had ever authored a book before joining our team! In fact, most of our authors never even considered writing a book prior to being on our team. But something happens when you join a family of creative thinkers: you become just like them!

> THE PEOPLE AROUND US AWAKEN THE DESTINIES DORMANT WITHIN US.

The people around us awaken the destinies dormant within us. Remember: if we find our people, then we will discover our destinies.

5

DISCOVERING YOUR PEOPLE

By now you might be saying, "All right, Kris, you've convinced me that I need to find my people, but how do I find them? And how do I know they are the right people?"

These are great questions. The answers to these questions might be a little harder to explain than they are to experience.

At some point, most of us have felt a sense of unity, harmony, and oneness in a community, among a people group, or on a team. Much like the nation of Israel that was made up of twelve distinct and diverse tribes, the people of God have a tribal DNA.

There is a remarkable phenomenon in physics called *resonance* that explains the sense we have when we meet our people. Scientists tell us that all matter vibrates at specific frequencies. Resonance occurs when an object's natural vibration frequency responds to an external stimulus of the same frequency. If you know an object's natural rate of vibration, you can make it vibrate without touching it. This is where we get such expressions as, "I really resonate with that guy," or, "I resonate with your idea." We're using a scientific expression to define an experience we have when we encounter an idea or a person we like. Metaphorically speaking, our matter vibrates at the same frequency as their matter.

Although this term is sometimes used improperly, the accurate connotation of *resonance* is that we are feeling something or experiencing something in common with a certain person, people group, or revelation. It's a connection we can't completely explain.

This is often the most common way we find our people. We have a sense of resonance with a community of people who seem to vibrate at the same spiritual frequency. We often think so much alike that we literally find ourselves finishing each other's sentences. Discovering people with similar DNA can feel as if we've met a twin brother who was separated from us at birth.

The reason we seem to resonate at the same frequency with certain people is that we view the world through the same lens, and thus we value the same things. The prophet Amos, while delivering a message about God's coming condemnation of the Israelites, put it like this: "Can two walk together, unless they are agreed?" (Amos 3:3 NKJV). God and Amos were in sync with one another: God did the punishing, and Amos told Israel it was Him doing it.

The apostle Paul encouraged his fellow Christians to be in sync with each other: "Now I exhort you, brethren, by the name of our Lord Jesus Christ, that you all agree and that there be no divisions among you, but that you be made complete in the same mind and in the same judgment" (1 Corinthians 1:10).

It's not about you finding people who view the world from a right-or-wrong perspective as much as it is about finding natural kinships within a diverse world of tribes. Tribal diversity is illustrated beautifully in the parables of Jesus when He describes the various aspects of the kingdom of God. In the same way that white light passing through a prism refracts to show the spectrum of color, Jesus revealed the multidimensional nature of the Kingdom through His "Kingdom parables" in the book of Matthew.

He highlighted the many aspects of God's kingdom and the role its citizens play in society through these parables. Discovering which descriptions of the Kingdom you most resonate with and then finding others who resonate with the same aspects of the Kingdom will help you find your people.

> IT'S NOT ABOUT YOU FINDING PEOPLE WHO VIEW THE WORLD FROM A RIGHT-OR-WRONG PERSPECTIVE AS MUCH AS IT IS ABOUT FINDING NATURAL KINSHIPS WITHIN A DIVERSE WORLD OF TRIBES.

Remember, success is often determined by being on the right bus with the right people who have a like passion and purpose.

Here are a few examples of the diversity of the Kingdom and the roles of its people. I suggest you reread all the parables of Jesus in light of this revelation and pay attention to the ones you relate to the most.

Leaven

Jesus said, "The kingdom of heaven is like leaven, which a woman took and hid in three pecks of flour until it was all leavened" (Matthew 13:33). This parable depicts the influence that a little bit of yeast (leaven) has on an entire lump of dough. Although leaven is almost undetectable in flour, it causes the entire bowl of dough to rise. So it is with much of the kingdom of God that is stealthy within society and influences the cultural mind-sets of our time.

Do you see yourself hidden in society, as wise as a serpent and as innocent as a dove? Do you view yourself doing ordinary things in extraordinary ways? Are your good works secretly causing society to rise like leaven in bread dough? Do you have a high level of passion to see society transformed? If you answer these questions affirmatively, then these values must shape the people you do life with.

For example, your people would be very mindful of the condition of their city and feel a sense of responsibility for its welfare. They wouldn't be protesters or demonstrators (although there is nothing wrong with that if it's carried out properly); instead, they would be active in the community as participants in the systems of society.

Much like Joseph and Daniel, they are God's influential secret agents, disguised as everyday people who are altering the mind-sets of their community toward the Kingdom. These people embrace such scriptures as, "Let your light shine before men in such a way that they may see your good works, and glorify your Father who is in heaven" (Matthew 5:16).

I am passionate about the leaven parable because it resonates with Bethel's DNA. In fact, we often use this parable at Bethel Church to describe our particular cultural perspective as well as our divine call. People who have more of the violent-men-take-the-Kingdom-by-force attitude often don't feel fully actualized in our environment because we refuse to be protestors who chuck rocks at the palace walls of society.

Merchants

How about this one? "The kingdom of heaven is like a merchant seeking fine pearls, and upon finding one pearl of great value, he went and sold all that he had and bought it" (Matthew 13:45–46).

Maybe the risk-taker in you connects with a Kingdom that has embarked on an exhilarating and dangerous journey to find one precious pearl worth a lifetime of wages. Do you find life in prosperity, in the high-risk, winner-takes-all game? Do you have a "need for speed," so to speak? Do you hate the predictable and the mundane, and long for adventure? Then explorers, adventurers, and forerunners might be your people.

I think this parable also helps to describe the risk-taking nature of our Bethel tribe. We are a community of believers who have a need for adventure and aren't too worried about failing. We often drive settlers and comfort seekers crazy. Things are always changing in our world, and just about the time our people get comfortable, we break camp and set out on the next quest.

Fishers of Men

"Again, the kingdom of heaven is like a net that was let down into the lake and caught all kinds of fish" (Matthew 13:47 NIV). Three of the disciples really related to this one: "He said to them, 'Follow Me, and I will make you fishers of men'" (Matthew 4:19).

Does your soul long to capture the hearts of people and inspire them to join the kingdom of heaven? Does compassion for the lost compel you to wake in the night with a burden so great that it oppresses your very being with passion too heavy to carry? Do tears overcome you as you stare into the empty eyes of children crushed under the weights of their sins? Then there is a strong possibility that these desires should guide your destiny.

My friends at Iris Global remind me of this parable. Heidi Baker, who leads this ministry along with her husband, Rolland, is so possessed with passion for lost souls that it wakes her in the night with groanings too deep for words. Heidi's motto, Stop for the One, is not a slogan on a placard somewhere; it defines the passion that burns in the bones of everyone who is a part of Iris Global. My friends are radicals who have left their boats to become fishers of men.

If this description raises your blood pressure and stokes the flame in your being, then you will probably find your people along the shores of lost humanity, fishing for the souls of men.

Landowners

Maybe you relate more to the business side of God; your pulse increases with anticipation as you listen to the Master describe

His world. "For the kingdom of heaven is like a landowner who went out early in the morning to hire laborers for his vineyard" (Matthew 20:1). As the Lord unfolds the parable of the landowner, the challenges of his business, and the descriptions of his employees, you find yourself basking in His insights and wondering at His wisdom. If this is true about you, then these aspirations are signs that you may have found your people.

A perfect example of this tribal perspective of the Kingdom is Andy Mason. He has a ministry called Heaven in Business. He and the community that has grown around him are this manifestation of the Kingdom. They spend their days dreaming, strategizing, plotting, and planning ways of displaying Jesus in the marketplace. Andy's ministry has inspired entrepreneurs to impact influential marketplace people, mirroring the way Solomon's reign impacted the queen of Sheba.

> When the queen of Sheba perceived all the wisdom of Solomon, the house that he had built, the food of his table, the seating of his servants, the attendance of his waiters and their attire, his cupbearers, and his stairway by which he went up to the house of the LORD, there was no more spirit in her. Then she said to the king, "It was a true report which I heard in my own land about your words and your wisdom. Nevertheless I did not believe the reports, until I came and my eyes had seen it. And behold, the half was not told me. You exceed in wisdom and prosperity the report which I heard. How blessed are your men, how blessed are these your servants who stand before you continually and hear your wisdom. Blessed be the LORD your God who delighted in you to set you on the throne of Israel;

because the LORD loved Israel forever, therefore He made you king, to do justice and righteousness." (1 Kings 10:4–9)

If these are the kinds of scriptures you dream about, if you resonate with the same sense of purpose to manifest God to people of influence, then find people with the same heart and collaborate with them.

Scriptures that Define You

The parables are not the only scriptures that help define us; many of us find ourselves resonating with other verses that mold and reveal our attitudes. As I mentioned earlier, I was saved in the Jesus Movement. The Jesus People were a countercultural group who lived communally, grew gardens, and ate off the land. Their motto was,

> "COME OUT FROM THEIR MIDST AND BE SEPARATE," says
> the Lord.
> "AND DO NOT TOUCH WHAT IS UNCLEAN;
> And I will welcome you."
>
> (2 CORINTHIANS 6:17)

It was an isolationist mind-set which, it turned out, was not me. Personally, I loved the Jesus People. We shared a heart for holiness and passion for God, but what they shouted (metaphorically speaking) I whispered, and what I shouted, they whispered. Although I admired them, and many of them are still my friends today, they are not my tribe. I wilted in the shade of their isolation-from-society tree. Their lack of motivation to transform the world drove me crazy. It was a constant point of conflict in our relationships, until I finally decided to move on.

One leaning is not necessarily better than the other, but it's important to identify which way you do lean when you are searching for your people. Here are a few more perspectives that may reveal more of who you are and who your people are.

CHILDLIKE

There is another kind of people I really admire. These are the childlike people who lead uncomplicated lives. It is fair to say that we are all called to be childlike. But for some, childlikeness is more than an attribute, it's a gene that defines them.

So let me ask you a few questions: Do you connect with the humility of the Lamb of God when He proclaimed, "Truly I say to you, whoever does not receive the kingdom of God like a child will not enter it at all" (Luke 18:17)? Do you have a profound sense of innocence and unwavering trust in God, His Word, and the people He's placed in your life? Do you prefer the simple life—a life that's not complicated by a lot of responsibility, ambitious pursuits, or great exploits but is instead characterized by unguarded love and relationship with those who are already naturally a part of your life? Is your heart's motto, "Why can't everyone just love one another and get along?"

If you are the kind of person who never really grew up but instead grew in—into Jesus, into His nature, into His virtues— then maybe you will find your people among this tribe: the people who have simple, uncomplicated faith.

RESPONSIBLE

On the other hand, some of you find yourselves resonating with the words of the apostle Paul when he said, "When I was a child, I used to speak like a child, think like a child, reason like a child; when I became a man, I did away with childish things" (1 Corinthians 13:11).

Maybe you are the kind of person who, while still embracing childlike humility, is driven to step out and meet the needs of the broken and hurting in a community. For you, responsibility is job number one! You understand that "love suffers long" (13:4 NKJV), and you feel fully actualized when you are in the fray, mourning with those who mourn and rejoicing with those who rejoice. You are the serious type who is always learning and growing. Having fun is sometimes the fruit of your experience, but it's never been your goal.

If this describes you, then you are more likely to find your people in the cornfield than at the ballfield, in the workplace than at the bowling alley.

SERVANT-MINDED

All believers are royalty and, simultaneously, servants of all. Yet some believers are more servant-minded in their natures than others. They exemplify the nature of the suffering Savior. They feel fully alive when they do practical things for people.

The Kingdom has a high value for the attributes of servant-hood. Jesus said, "If anyone wants to be first, he shall be last of all and servant of all" (Mark 9:35). Your seat of servanthood is your throne of destiny.

My wife Kathy is a great example of these attributes. She

would rather pray than preach, serve dinner than dialogue with the mighty. Although she has great self-esteem, she thinks as a servant and serves as a queen.

Ask yourself these questions: Is your passion activated through service? Do you naturally think about meeting the needs of people? Do you envision yourself joining others in coordinated efforts to touch the poor or help the broken?

If these things are true about you, then these values must be resident in your people in order for you to resonate with them.

NOBLE

Some of you just reek of royalty. You carry yourself nobly and come across as if you work in the White House or someplace equally as grandiose. The apostle Paul said, "You are already filled, you have already become rich, you have become kings without us; and indeed, I wish that you had become kings so that we also might reign with you" (1 Corinthians 4:8).

Do you carry yourself with nobility and dream of discipling influencers? Or do you envision yourself leading in some arena with a team of top-tier advisors? Do you see yourself more like King David or King Solomon than Joseph or Daniel (who advised kings)? If this is you, you are more likely to meet your people in the community than in the congregation.

I have a few noble friends who are like this. They have great favor and divine insight to solve complex world problems. They are more like eagles than geese in that they don't tend to flock together. Their worlds are often a little isolated, and they sometimes struggle attending church because the congregation is inclined to pull on them in unhealthy ways. Because of this, they are prone not to trust a lot of people. They tend to be really friendly, but it can also be very hard to connect with them. So, ultimately, nobility comes at a cost.

If you resonate with these attributes, then these are your people. It will be important for you to press past your desire to be alone so you can have deep relational connections with these like-minded people.

BRIDE-LIKE

The Song of Solomon is the story of two lovers who are so passionate about each other that they make their readers blush. Let's read a small sample of the book so you can catch the essence of the people who fall into this bride-like tribe:

> May he kiss me with the kisses of his mouth!
> For your love is better than wine.
>
> Your oils have a pleasing fragrance,
> Your name is like purified oil;
> Therefore the maidens love you.
>
> Draw me after you and let us run together!
> The king has brought me into his chambers.
>
> (SONG OF SOLOMON 1:2–4)

Is this you? Are you a hopeless romantic? Are you so constantly caught up in romancing the Bridegroom that it seems the rest of life is a bother? Do you value feelings and experiences above tasks and accomplishments? Is your life the very depiction of Song of Solomon: lovers enthralled and captivated by passion? Do you relate to God both as Creator and Lover?

If you answered affirmatively, then passion is the hallmark of your tribal DNA. You probably approach life as the bride does and express yourself through creativity; it's common to find your tribe in a community of artists, musicians, or dancers—people known for being sensitive, intuitive, prophetic, and creative.

COMPETITIVE

I really admire this next tribe. These folks are the Holy Spirit Olympians! They view life as a cross-country race. They seem to be training constantly for the "big day." They are disciplined and intense, and consequently they have little time for small talk. For these folks, a minute wasted is a race lost. They live with such intention that it drives most people around them nuts. These people don't watch TV; they read nonfiction books. They view the Bible as a training manual that is to be memorized and proactively implemented. Their conversations consist of strategic plans and lofty goals.

Paul summed up this lifestyle when he wrote to the church at Corinth, "Do you not know that those who run in a race all run, but only one receives the prize? Run in such a way that you may win" (1 Corinthians 9:24). Is this you? Do you feel that life is a competition waiting to be won or an obstacle course that must be conquered?

I must admit I am often a little intimidated by the mere discipline of these people. They can be so regimented that they sometimes view everybody else as lazy or complacent. They can also find themselves competing with everyone, including their friends. But these people are usually the backbone of any organization. Whatever they lack in talent, they make up for in effort. They tend to be the hardest workers in the community. Their motto seems to be, "If you want a relationship with us, then come run with us."

If this describes you, your people will probably be found at a basketball court, gym, or in the outback somewhere climbing a mountain—in any environment with activities requiring intense discipline.

BATTLE-READY

The battle-ready are as intense and regimented as the disciplined athletes, yet for them life isn't a race, it's a war! They view the world as a battlefield and see themselves as soldiers who are engaged in an intense struggle against the devil for the souls of men. They live in a constant fight, wrestling and warring with principalities and powers.

The apostle Paul was definitely the personification of a soldier. His many imprisonments, stonings, and beatings probably shaped this mentality in him. Paul seemed to require those who accompanied him to enlist in his "armed forces." This is evidenced in his exhortation to Timothy when he wrote, "Suffer hardship with me, as a good soldier of Christ Jesus. No soldier in active service entangles himself in the affairs of everyday life, so that he may please the one who enlisted him as a soldier" (2 Timothy 2:3–4).

Paul had very little patience for the civilian attitude, which was evidenced by his conflict with his good friend and ministry partner Barnabas. When Barnabas wanted Mark to accompany them on their second missionary journey, Paul blatantly refused to take him. Evidently Mark got scared and went AWOL on their first missionary exploit, so Paul had no intention of taking that coward with him again. The argument became so heated that Barnabas finally went on alone with Mark, while Paul partnered with Silas.

Hanging around warriors can be exhilarating if you are one of them, or exhausting if you are not. My friend David Hogan, who works with the indigenous people deep in the jungles of Mexico, leads a tribe of people like this. His staff has an intense regimen, which they are required to submit to. They fast three days a week, work out every day, and run several miles a week. They are intense, tough, and bold. They view the devil as the powerful foe with whom they are engaged in a daily struggle. They have no time for silliness or patience for complacency. Theirs is a world at war in which violent men take the kingdom by force.

Maybe you were born to be a soldier, but somehow you never genuinely enlisted in the army of God. You exist in a constant state of frustration, because the believers around you live a life of leisure while the battle rages right next to them. To make matters worse, the louder and longer you sound the alarm the further you find yourself from community camp, until finally one day you are all by yourself. Is this you? Perhaps you just caught the wrong bus!

HARDWORKING

While some people are soldiers, still others are hardworking farmers. For them, life is about land, fruit trees, and fertilizer. Farmers are plodders; they are consistent and patient people who, through prolonged labor, receive their rewards in harvest seasons. Paul shared this observation about them: "The hard-working farmer ought to be the first to receive his share of the crops" (2 Timothy 2:6–7).

Skilled farmers must be visionaries because they plant trees that yield no harvest for several years. I learned this lesson from my grandfather, who raised me. The price of peaches plummeted when I was in high school, so my grandfather and I pulled all of them out and planted walnut trees. What I didn't understand at the time was that the walnut trees we planted would bear nothing worth harvesting for five long years. Looking back now, I understand that farmers are people who are constantly investing in the future. They labor in hope and live by faith, dreaming of a better day.

Perhaps you find yourself at home among these folk. You love to work hard, and you exhibit great patience, knowing your effort will be rewarded in time. You enjoy doing life in different seasons. You love to chill in the winter of life, aware that "He who gathers in summer is a son who acts wisely, but he who sleeps in harvest is a son who acts shamefully" (Proverbs 10:5).

Bus Stops

Now that we've talked about a few of the common tribal attributes, hopefully you have a clearer idea of what bus you should catch. I created these lists to help you recognize your people when you meet them at the bus stops of life. I want to challenge you to put your tribal glasses on when you read your Bible. Look for the kingdom attributes and attitudes your heart resonates with as you comb through its pages. Pay attention to the DNA within you so you can discover your people in the world around you. Remember: until you find your people, you can't fully apprehend your divine destiny because your destiny lies in your people!

6

SURROUNDED BY IDIOTS

We have already spent a good amount of time talking about finding your people and boarding the right bus, but even the right bus has some wrong people on it, and every great family has a crazy uncle. Therefore, it's imperative that you proactively decide whom you give access to your heart. The fact is, the people who are allowed to influence you will determine whether you become a world-changer or a miserable failure! You read me right: if you surround yourself with idiots, you will become just like them. Too harsh, you say? Consider these proverbs:

> He who walks with wise men will be wise,
> But the companion of fools will suffer harm.
>
> (PROVERBS 13:20)

I love how *The Message* puts it:

> Become wise by walking with the wise;
> hang out with fools and watch your life fall to pieces.
>
> Leave the presence of a fool,
> Or you will not discern words of knowledge.
>
> (PROVERBS 14:7)

We may not say it the same way, but we all know this instinctively. We have all said things like, "He's a good kid; he just got in with the wrong crowd." That's right, the wrong crowd can wreak havoc on a good kid. The apostle Paul said it best: "Bad company corrupts good morals" (1 Corinthians 15:33).

Lost in Space

God promised the children of Israel a land flowing with milk and honey, but the people refused to believe Him. Consequently, all of them, except for two, died in the wilderness. What's the moral of the story? It's simple: if you hang around the wrong people and let them influence you, then your promises may be delayed or even deleted.

Joshua and Caleb are perfect examples of two guys who were faithful. They both loved God, and they believed in their divine destinies, but they entered their promised land forty years late because they hung around with fools. The truth is, they had to wait until the last fool died off before they could even set one foot on their promised territory.

Let me be clear: we are all called to help the poor, love the needy, and heal the brokenhearted—no matter what condition we find them in. We all know that. We are also aware that Jesus hung out with sinners. In fact, some of His own disciples were not the sharpest knives in the drawer. But there is a big difference between ministering to people and letting them influence you.

"Oh, Kris, this just doesn't feel Christlike!"

Well, maybe your perspective of Jesus needs to be expanded. Consider what Jesus said to some of the religious leaders of His day:

> Woe to you, scribes and Pharisees, hypocrites, because you travel around on sea and land to make one proselyte; and when he becomes one, you make him twice as much a son of hell as yourselves.
>
> Woe to you, blind guides, who say, "Whoever swears by the temple, that is nothing; but whoever swears by the gold of the temple is obligated." You fools and blind men! Which is more important, the gold or the temple that sanctified the gold? (Matthew 23:15–17)

Whether you like it or not, Jesus confronted fools. He certainly didn't have a ton of patience for them. To be clear, I share a harsh quote from Jesus just to remind you that He didn't pull punches with people who were enslaving others with their lies. But I am not talking about being harsh; I am talking about inviting honesty, not foolishness, into your inner circle.

Nowadays, under the guise of free speech, people spew the most foolish, ridiculous nonsense without so much as a kind rebuttal.

For instance, women are no longer carrying babies. They are pregnant with a fetus which, consequently, is only human if she decides to give birth to it! If it's aborted, even in the third trimester, it's only tissue. What?

Personally, I would rather be right than be politically correct. We owe the world the truth. It's the truth that sets people free! If the truth sets you free, then it must be lies that imprison you. So, as you're considering who to invite into your life, note the difference between people who speak what is popular and people who speak what is true.

The Art of Taking Counsel

How do you avoid being bound by lies? You learn to take counsel from the right people. Let's say you've avoided allowing foolish people to speak into your life. Great! But if you create a culture around you where truth-telling is costly, you will silence your wisest counselors. I can't tell you how many times people have invited me to speak into their lives and then later punished me for my opinion.

If you want to be a world-changer, you will need to learn the art of taking advice. If you ask for input and then argue with the people who are counseling you, you are sending them a clear message that you don't value what they have to say.

The other way you send that message is by giving them the silent treatment after they advise you. When you pout or avoid your advisors after they have shared their opinions with you, you can bet they'll think twice before they ever advise you again.

Here are five questions you can ask yourself that will reveal if you are acting like a fool or carrying yourself in wisdom:

1. Are you a know-it-all who thinks that you are always right, or do you instinctively and intuitively ask for input?

> The way of a fool is right in his own eyes,
> But a wise man is he who listens to counsel.
>
> (PROVERBS 12:15)

2. Do you let people correct you, or are you hardheaded?

> A fool rejects his father's discipline,
> But he who regards reproof is sensible.
>
> (PROVERBS 15:5)

3. When someone is giving you input that you don't like, are you thinking of your rebuttal while he or she is talking, or are you listening from the heart?

> A fool does not delight in understanding,
> But only in revealing his own mind.
>
> (PROVERBS 18:2)

4. Is talking to you a big waste of time because you never change, or do you actually act on wise people's advice?

> Though you pound a fool in a mortar with a pestle along
> with crushed grain,

Yet his foolishness will not depart from him.

(PROVERBS 27:22)

5. Are you overconfident, arrogant, and egotistical; or are you humble, teachable, and able to be influenced?

He who trusts in his own heart is a fool,
But he who walks wisely will be delivered.

(PROVERBS 28:26)

The Truth Hurts

Let's be honest, sometimes the truth really does hurt. Proverbs says,

Faithful are the wounds of a friend,
But deceitful are the kisses of an enemy.

(27:6)

Your counselors may not always be right, yet the Bible says, "in abundance of counselors there is victory" (Proverbs 11:14). Every world-changer must create a culture of invitation, where wise people are proactively invited to speak into your life whenever they perceive it's necessary and also when you ask for it.

Did you notice there are two different times when wise people should speak into your life? First and foremost, when you ask for counsel; and second, when they see something in your life that you don't see. Think about it: if you create a culture around you in which wise people can only give you advice when you ask for it, then you will never get past your blind spots. Obviously, you don't see or perceive your blind spots; that's why they're called blind spots.

It's often in the places where you are unconsciously ignorant (you don't know that you don't know) that you actually need the most input.

> IT'S OFTEN IN THE PLACES WHERE YOU ARE UNCONSCIOUSLY IGNORANT THAT YOU ACTUALLY NEED THE MOST INPUT.

A Foolish King

The biblical character who probably squandered the greatest opportunity by ignoring counsel was King Solomon's son, Rehoboam. He was born with a silver spoon in his mouth, his grandfather being the famous King David and his father being the wisest man who ever walked the earth. Yet Rehoboam was an idiot king because he rejected the advice of his wise counselors and instead listened to his foolish friends. Ultimately he lost his authority.

> King Rehoboam consulted with the elders who had served his father Solomon while he was still alive, saying, "How do you counsel me to answer this people?" Then they spoke to him, saying, "If you will be a servant to this people today, and will serve them and grant them their petition, and speak

good words to them, then they will be your servants forever." But he forsook the counsel of the elders which they had given him, and consulted with the young men who grew up with him and served him. So he said to them, "What counsel do you give that we may answer this people who have spoken to me, saying, 'Lighten the yoke which your father put on us'?" The young men who grew up with him spoke to him, saying, "Thus you shall say to this people who spoke to you, saying, 'Your father made our yoke heavy, now you make it lighter for us!' But you shall speak to them, 'My little finger is thicker than my father's loins! Whereas my father loaded you with a heavy yoke, I will add to your yoke; my father disciplined you with whips, but I will discipline you with scorpions.'" (1 Kings 12:6–11)

And so the king answered the people harshly, forsaking the advice of the elders and following the advice of his buddies, saying, "My father made your yoke heavy, but I will add to your yoke; my father disciplined you with whips, but I will discipline you with scorpions" (1 Kings 12:14). This began the rebellion of Israel against the house of David.

Rehoboam had an opportunity to be a part of an amazing legacy called the United Kingdom of Israel, which began when King David unified all the Israelite tribes under one king and which extended through the reign of Solomon. But Rehoboam listened to the fools he grew up with instead of his time-tested elders. Ultimately, he squandered the opportunity of the ages and will forever be known as the king who broke Israel in half.

Build a Wise Counsel around You

I have a friend named Doug Coe who is the director of a believer's organization called the Fellowship. He has been referred to as the "stealth Billy Graham." In 2005, Doug was named one of the twenty-five most influential evangelicals in the United States by *Time*.[1] He has counseled world leaders and may be one of the wisest men alive today. In 1990, at the National Prayer Breakfast, President George H. W. Bush praised Coe for his "quiet diplomacy."[2]

Hillary Clinton met with Coe on many occasions during her time as the First Lady of the United States. Clinton has written that Doug Coe is "a unique presence in Washington: a genuinely loving spiritual mentor and guide to anyone, regardless of party or faith, who wants to deepen his or her relationship with God."[3] Former Vice President Al Gore has referred to Doug Coe as a "friend."[4]

Last year I had the privilege of introducing two world leaders to Doug. One of them was the mayor of one of the largest cities in America, and the other was the leader of a foreign country. We made small talk for a while, and then one of my two friends asked Doug a question. "What advice do you give most often to world leaders?"

Without a second of hesitation Doug responded, "I have studied world leaders all my life, and I have found that the great ones all have one thing in common. Do you know what it is?"

We all shook our heads and motioned for him to continue.

"Well," Doug said with his matter-of-fact demeanor, "They

have all developed a wise counsel of people around them who advised them all their lives. That is the secret to success: assemble a company of smart, experienced, and wise people around you and invite them to speak into everything you do."

My friends left that day determined to build their own teams of wise counselors.

Meet Our Dream Team

By the grace of God, I have been blessed with a world-class dream team. God has empowered us to influence the world together. Several of us have been walking alongside each other for more than thirty-seven years. This kind of longevity gives us unique perspectives on one another's lives. We know each other's flaws, weaknesses, and failures well; but more importantly, we have a great understanding of one another's strengths, expertise, and places of competent wisdom.

If you knew us, you would probably wonder how we stay in the same room together, much less collaborate on the same team, because we are all so incredibly different. Let me introduce some of our team to you.

There is Bill Johnson, who is the deeply spiritual leader of our team. He is a fifth-generation pastor who kind of reminds me of Moses. He speaks to God face-to-face (or at least it seems that way). He is a serious internal processer who is prone to not say much, but like E. F. Hutton, when he speaks, everybody listens. His ability to perceive life from heaven's perspective is uncanny.

I think Charlie Harper has been with us since the dinosaurs

became extinct. He is quiet like Bill, but his wheels are always turning. He is educated, and he grew up in the banking and real estate worlds. Charles is wise with money, and he actually loves reading legal documents. Yuck! He is methodical and patient, so he is great at managing projects . . . such as our $60 million building project he is leading right now. He is also extremely diplomatic; he thinks long and hard before he opens his mouth (not a trait I possess, unfortunately).

Steve De Silva is our anchor. He has great faith but hates taking risks! Steve is usually the one who challenges the visionaries on our team the most. He is a licensed CPA, and he is our chief financial officer. He is the point man on Bethel's multimillion-dollar budget. Steve is highly educated in corporate tax law and is an excellent people manager. He loves to process vocally, but he rarely does so unless someone invites him to give his input.

Kathy Vallotton is a world-class administrator. She can figure out how to accomplish anything. I believe she could run the entire country. Kathy is the only true executor on our senior leadership team (I am not talking about killing people. I mean she is our get-'er-done leader). She can drive us nuts with practical questions the rest of us wouldn't think to ask if you left us alone in a room for ten years. She oversees the entire administration of our ministry school, which has more than two thousand full-time students and an $8.4 million budget.

Paul Manwaring is our British guy. I just like listening to him talk. He is an amazing strategist who thinks that most of the problems in the world can be solved with a strategic plan. He was a psychiatric nurse before he was the governor of a juvenile prison in England, where he earned top honors. I guess God felt Paul needed that kind of training to thrive on our team! He gets along with everybody; he knows no strangers. He oversees our network of churches called Global Legacy, among other things.

Then there's Dann Farrelly. How do I describe Dann to you? Well, to begin with, he is the brightest and most highly educated person on our team. He is our theologian and historian; I guess you could say he is our Bible guy. Curiously enough, he's probably one of the least ambitious leaders I have ever met. I don't think I have ever seen him compete with anyone. Dann, unlike some of our team, loves to process verbally and is respected by everyone.

Eric and Candace Johnson are the senior leaders of our church of eight thousand people. They are young, hip, and forward thinking. They both have strong personalities and are also ambitious, capable, and exceptionally creative leaders. Eric and Candace are sincerely passionate about people, especially families. Eric has what I call a "persistent pursuit of excellence." He always wants to get it right and do it perfectly.

Brian Johnson is quiet, like his father, Bill. He is prophetic and forward thinking. He is the founder of Bethel Music, an artist, a musician, and a writer. Brian is sensitive, and he speaks with great authority. He and his wife, Jenn, have a hundred artists and musicians on their team, which is a lot like herding cats.

And last but not least there is Danny Silk (who formerly pastored Mountain Chapel and a few years later joined us at Bethel Church). Danny is like our team psychologist. He has an extraordinary gift for understanding what motivates people, what lie at the roots of their challenges and struggles. He is famous for getting between us in times of conflict and helping us to understand one another. He always takes the lead whenever there are people problems in our organization or congregation.

Now add me to the mix, and you have a recipe for disaster—or the *Mission: Impossible* team, depending on how we choose to conduct ourselves. I am a verbal processor; I come to conclusions by talking things out, which sometimes means I am not committed to the ideas that I seem passionate about at first. (Sometimes this drives our team crazy.) I am an extreme risk taker who is a prophetic visionary, entrepreneur, and builder. I have a great passion and love for people, but sometimes I am impatient and not compassionate. In my pursuit to accomplish a task or fulfill a goal, I can unknowingly run over people. Without this team around me, I think my life would be a trail of tears.

I truly love our team! Through the years I have learned that the strength of any leader lies in his or her ability to attract and keep very capable people around. The challenge is that we don't tend to draw the people we want (or need); we are more likely to attract the people who are like us. This can be a good thing in that our team needs to have shared core values, DNA, and vision. Yet we need people with diverse gifts, perspectives, and abilities.

Here is the challenge: if, for instance, you are really bad with money, it can be hard to hang out with wealthy people who know how to steward finances. This is true for a couple of reasons. First, the mere contrast of being around people who have money tends to remind you of your poor condition. Second, you probably don't have the financial capability to participate in the activities that wealthy people can afford to do. Yet the only way to learn how to overcome your weaknesses is to hang out with people who are good at the things you are bad at. Therefore, you must brave the pain of contrast and proactively solicit the assistance of great leaders. This is the key to building a world-class team!

The DTR Dance

If you assemble the right kinds of people around you, that strong council of capable people will help you become tremendously successful. The good thing about choosing a strong team is that you will receive lots of great advice when you need it. The bad thing about this team is that you will receive lots of great advice when the members think you need it. No, that's not a typo. The truth is, if you surround yourself with weaker people, you probably won't have much trouble managing them. On the other hand, if you assemble a strong team and give fellow members permission to speak into your life, you might feel that they are controlling you instead of advising you. Therefore, there will always come a time when it will be necessary to *define the relationship* (DTR).

> THE FOUNDATION OF ALL RELATIONSHIPS, WHETHER PERSONAL OR CORPORATE, IS TRUST. TRUST IS BUILT WHEN WE CREATE EXPECTATIONS THAT WE FULFILL.

Let me explain. The foundation of all relationships, whether personal or corporate, is trust. Trust is built when we create expectations that we fulfill. But too often, whether consciously or unconsciously, we create expectations that we never fulfill. This results in a history of broken relationships and ultimately leads to a life of regret. Most of this destructive conduct can be avoided by an honest DTR.

When we define our relationships with people, we give each other honest assessments of what we can expect from one another. This begins the dialogue that ultimately leads to an agreement of what we are willing to do (and be) and not do (and be) in the lives of one another. Thus our relationships are built on solid foundations of trust that give us confidence in our interactions with each other.

Besides marriage, I can't think of any other type of relationship that is more important to define than the one you have with your Council of Leaders (COL).

Here are seven core values and seven relationship definitions that must be present for your COL to be fully actualized in your life:

1. Core value: *Everyone must carry a can of gasoline and a pail of water.* The goal must be to surround yourself with people who will pour gasoline on the fires of your dreams and drench the flames of your fears with water.

   DTR—Make it clear to your potential COL candidates that you are not looking for dream killers or fear mongers. Let them know that you have specifically chosen them because they are wise, full of faith, and have proven character.

2. Core value: *The team must cultivate a culture of honor.* Honor means that you value each other for who you are, without stumbling over who you are not. Honor dictates the way you behave in your interactions with each

other, especially in your conflicts. Honor demands that you show one another a high level of respect when you disagree, as well as when you agree. Honor doesn't control people; the idea that "if you honored my counsel then you would do what I told you to do," is just a smoke screen for manipulation. Honor values the rights of others to control themselves. Remember, although God is in charge, He refuses to be in control of us. Yes, God has a sovereign plan, but He uses freewill agents to accomplish it.

DTR—Make it clear to your potential COL candidates how honor looks to you. Describe to them how honor behaves in different scenarios: How does honor behave in disagreements? How does honor convey wise counsel? What does honor require when someone is being corrected? How does honor affect the way you listen to the new ideas of others? When someone fails, how does honor pick that person up? How do you honorably clean up your messes with one another?

3. Core value: *The COL must intentionally draw out the deep things of God in each other and then help to activate them in one another.* Proverbs tells us,

> A plan in the heart of a man is like deep water,
> But a man of understanding draws it out. (20:5)

One of the best examples of biblical accountability is the relationship that the apostle Paul had with his spiritual son, Timothy. Look closely at the exhortation he gave to Timothy in this letter:

Let no one look down on your youthfulness, but
rather in speech, conduct, love, faith and purity, show
yourself an example of those who believe. . . . Do
not neglect the spiritual gift within you, which was
bestowed on you through prophetic utterance with
the laying on of hands by the presbytery. Take pains
with these things; be absorbed in them, so that your
progress will be evident to all. Pay close attention
to yourself and to your teaching; persevere in these
things, for as you do this you will ensure salvation
both for yourself and for those who hear you.
(1 Timothy 4:12, 13–16)

Here is a summary of what Paul was holding Timothy
accountable for:

- *Don't let people look down on you.* Did you get the
  "don't let them" concept? That comment alone should
  stimulate some exciting conversation with your team!
- *Carry yourself like nobility.* That certainly shoots the
  "don't follow me, follow Jesus," idea in the head!
- *You received some special spiritual gifts through
  impartation. Be diligent to grow what was freely given to
  you.* Enough said.
- *Work your butt off until you get really good at using
  your gifts to build up others around you. In fact, I want
  everyone around you to see your progress.* The idea that
  you should show up and show off so that people
  around you can see and be encouraged by how good
  you are at the stuff that was given to you pretty much

flies in the face of everything we have been taught in
church about humility.

• *Pay attention to yourself and to your teaching, so
wholeness will live in you and flow through you to those
around you.* Wow! Have you ever thought about how
important it is to God that you take care of you?

Paul's instructions to Timothy almost seem self-
serving, but the truth is, if you don't take care of yourself,
then the people you are called to lead and serve will
pay. On the other hand, when you live in community,
everyone in relationship with you benefits from your
maturity.

DTR—Make sure everyone on your COL team
has a sense of mutual accountability. But remember
accountability is giving an account for your ability, not
for your disability. I love how Paul Manwaring put
it: "Accountability isn't making sure someone doesn't
smoke. It's actually helping to make sure they are on
fire." I am not saying members of your COL shouldn't
honorably confront one another when they feel it's
necessary; they really should. I am simply pointing
out that the purpose of this team isn't to give you
a character MRI every time you meet. You are not
gathering a team of faultfinders who use their gifts of
discernment to scan each other's hearts and examine
each other's motives every time you gather. Rather, your
default should be to discover, develop, and empower the
gifts, callings, and anointings that are resident in each
member of the team.

4. Core value: *Ownership is the key to successful exploits in life.* John Maxwell quotes Vince Pfaff in his book *JumpStart Your Leadership*: "People tend to resist that which is forced upon them. People tend to support that which they help create."[5] One of the best ways to build synergy with a team of people is through collaboration. True collaboration requires your team to have a sense of ownership in the decisions you make and in the things you build together.

The truth is, what some people call teamwork is a lot more like slavery. When one person is doing all the thinking while the rest are just carrying out tasks, that's not teamwork; that is a monarchy. This kind of leadership is rampant in the church. Great teams don't behave this way! To reach your team's full potential, you will have to develop plans with them, not for them.

You can tell those who have bought in, because they use inclusive words when they describe the team's activities. For instance, when they feel a sense of ownership they use words such as *us*, *we*, and *our*, instead of *you*, *your*, and *their* to articulate the undertakings of the team.

In order to have others buy-in and collaborate, it may be necessary for you to adjust the way you present your ideas to your COL. Nothing feels worse than someone asking for my opinion when that person has already made up his mind what he is going to do, and all he really wants is my stamp of approval. Therefore, when you have something in your mind that you really want to see happen, try to leave room in your heart to adjust your idea or even scrap it.

I am struck by the phrase that is used in the book of Acts to describe how the apostles came to decisions. Luke wrote, "It seemed good to us, *having become of one mind,* to select men to send to you with our beloved Barnabas and Paul" (Acts 15:25, emphasis added). The connotation is that the apostles dialogued until they came to an agreement. In fact, this is exactly how Acts 15 describes the discussion that the apostles had concerning how the Gentiles should relate to the law of Moses.

One of the ways I get our team to buy-in is to offer my idea as a question. This gives our team members permission to share their thoughts without feeling as if they are killing me. It also ultimately helps me to see my concept from several different perspectives without feeling that I have to defend myself.

> "GOD IDEAS" WILL STAND THE SCRUTINY OF FAITH-FILLED PEOPLE, BUT GOOD IDEAS TYPICALLY WON'T.

Bill Johnson uses a different approach; he will throw out an idea and say, "Tell me why this won't work." Either way, the outcome is the same. Everyone feels empowered to share his or her perspective with the team. What I have discovered over the years is that "God ideas" will stand the scrutiny of faith-filled people, but good ideas typically won't.

DTR—It's important for your COL to understand that whenever your team accomplishes anything, the entire team shares the credit, no matter who came up with the idea. If we win, we win together; and when we lose, we lose together.

Another thing that is essential to understanding the team dynamic is that everyone has an equal voice, but not everyone on your team has an equal vote all the time. What I mean is that certain COL members' opinions will carry more weight at times, especially when that person has experience or expertise in the specific area you are addressing. In this way you are honoring the gift that's on a person's life by acknowledging that, under certain circumstances, his or her opinion carries more authority on the team.

For example, I may be in charge of a certain project; but if a relational issue comes up in the midst of trying to accomplish a task, I almost always defer my authority to Danny Silk because he is more gifted in this area than I am, as is anyone else on our team, for that matter.

5. Core Value: *Being a part of a team and making decisions together means that nobody always gets his or her way.* Therefore it's important that you don't allow the I-told-you-so syndrome to take root in your team. Once a decision is made, no matter who was for it or who was against it, everyone is obligated to do his or her best in two things:

i. Present a united front to everyone your team is influencing and leading. It's not okay for anyone on your COL to let others know that he or she disagreed with the team's ultimate decision. This is divisive, undermining, and confusing. This kind of behavior must be confronted.

ii. Everyone on the team must do everything in his or her power to help the decision that was made by the team to succeed. Can you imagine being on a sports team and having the coach call a play that you didn't like, so you just refused to participate in the play? That would be a quick way to get benched and ultimately kicked off the team.

DTR—Be clear when you are bringing people onto your team that you must have a united front even if things don't go their way. I learned the hard way that some very gifted people are just not team players for various reasons. Some of them are so needy that they want all the credit for everything. This, of course, destroys collaboration and hamstrings any team dynamic. Then there are people who just don't have the relational skills to play well with others. Their low Emotional Quotient is so distracting that it undermines any benefit they bring to the team.

With this in mind, I would suggest that you bring a person onto your COL team for a maximum of a year to start with. If the person fits well with the team, then you can extend his or her role as you see fit.

6. Core Value: *Diversity is the key to success on any great team.* It's imperative that you find people from your tribe (or on your bus) who have different gifts and perspectives than you have; otherwise you are creating the clone zone. The challenge is that we are often uncomfortable with people

who think differently than we do. We have a hard time understanding how they can see the same problem we see and yet come to completely different conclusions about how to solve it.

Author Doris Goodwin captures this concept of diversity in her bestselling book entitled *Team of Rivals*. It's the true story of Abraham Lincoln's diverse leadership team. Goodwin makes the case for Lincoln's political genius by examining his relationships with three men he selected for his cabinet, all of whom were opponents for the Republican nomination in 1860: William H. Seward, Salmon P. Chase, and Edward Bates. These men—all accomplished, nationally known, and presidential— originally disdained Lincoln for his backwoods upbringing and lack of experience. Yet Lincoln not only convinced them to join his administration—Seward as secretary of state, Chase as secretary of the treasury, and Bates as attorney general—but he ultimately gained their admiration and respect. How he soothed their egos, turned rivals into allies, and dealt with many challenges to his leadership (all for the sake of the greater good) is largely what Goodwin's fine book is about. Had Lincoln not possessed the wisdom and confidence to select and work with the best people, she argues, he could not have led the nation through one of its darkest periods.[6]

Remember, unity is not conformity; it's a celebration of diversity. The apostle Paul had real insights into believers working together when he wrote, "For just as we have many members in one body and all the members do not have the same function, so we, who are many, are one body in Christ, and individually members of one another" (Romans 12:4–5). Reread that last clause: we are "individually members of one another" We must create a leadership culture where the members of our COL don't lose their senses of identity and individuality for the sake of unity. Like Lincoln, our genius is in building a team of diverse people who can work together for the common good.

DTR—Let your team know the importance of having a high level of honor and value for one another, especially in the midst of your diversity. There is an old saying: "If you walk in my shoes then you will understand how I think." One of the best ways to learn to value others is to truly get to know them. Whenever you consider adding someone to your COL, let the other members get to know that person first. In other words, court before you marry. When you're courting, proactively challenge your team to discover the potential candidate's true identity, as well as his or her greatest accomplishments. It's funny to me that when you ask most men *who* they are, they will tell you *what* they do. What you do is important, but why you do it and how you do it is much more revealing.

7. Core Value. *Visionaries and administrators working collaboratively are necessary for success.* Visionaries are the architects of your destiny. Administrators, on the other hand, are your builders, your get-it-done team. But getting visionaries and administrators to work together on

the same project is miraculous at best, and impossible for most teams.

The challenge is that visionaries are not always grounded in reality; they are often trying to turn water into wine. On the other hand, administrators are frequently trying to turn wine into water by reducing the vision to something that takes no faith to accomplish.

I have been in more meetings then I care to remember where visionaries and administrators were shouting at one another over a project. The truth is, you can envision anything you want as long as you don't actually have to do it or build it. It costs you nothing to envision a billion-dollar project in the name of faith. But what often follows "faith ventures" is a trail of tears as the visionary shames those who "refuse to believe God."

Conversely, I've been in many meetings where someone began to articulate a vision, only to be interrupted by the administrators who start telling them all the reasons it can't work—we don't have the money, we don't have the time, the people won't get behind it, yada, yada, yada!

Paul Manwaring said, "Administration means add to the mission." Most of the time we are not asking administrators if we should build something as much as we are asking them how to get it done. To truly realize what's been envisioned, we need administrators to operate at the same level of faith as the visionaries do, and we need the visionaries to heed the counsel of the administrators. Nothing great was ever built without visionaries, but nothing at all was ever built without administrators!

DTR—So the world-changing question is, how do you get administrators and visionaries to collaborate? First, you must develop envisioning meetings in which the visionaries are empowered to proactively, externally process their visions while administrators observe, listen, and receive. If the administrators cannot hold their tongues during these imagining sessions, then they should not be allowed into the meetings.

Next, call everyone together, and let the visionaries clearly articulate the vision to the administrators so they can capture the vision and personalize the mission. Afterward, send the administrators away, and task them with developing plans, goals, and steps to apprehend the vision. Have them make a list of the questions they have for the visionaries and send it to them.

Finally, gather everyone for an administrative meeting in which the visionaries congregate to answer questions posed to them by the get-it-done team. Everyone should be in "negotiate mode" when they gather. The main goal of this meeting is to clarify and establish the priorities of the visionaries. As the administrators articulate the cost and the challenges of the plan, as well as the process of apprehending the mission, the visionaries should weigh in on the importance level of certain characteristics of the vision. The administrators should also grasp the worthiness (or lack thereof) of the costly aspects of the mission.

There will always be compromises when you do or build anything great. That's why it's important for collaboration to take place among the dreamers and builders. Sometimes the builders want to diminish or cut something that isn't negotiable in the hearts of the visionaries. Other times things cost a lot of money and have very little impact on the overall scope of the mission. Unless there's an infinite amount of money, the administrators might be wise to eliminate or downgrade these sorts of extravagant extras.

Be Proactive

For the first twenty years of my life, most of the high-impact relationships I had happened organically. I had no strategy, plan, or mission to surround myself with a wise council of leaders. As a matter of fact, in my younger years I wasn't smart enough to understand the impact that prudent people could have on my life.

As I shared earlier in this book, I was fortunate to have "accidently" connected to Bill Johnson, who has been surrounded by great people for his entire life. Consequently, I benefited from the wise people who were following Bill, but it was mostly through osmosis.

Now that I'm older, I realize that great leaders proactively build relationships with wise people; they don't just wait for them to happen. As I have already stated in several ways, your destiny is determined by who is in you and who is around you. So I exhort you: make some wise friends, and transform your destiny!

7

TAKE YOUR PLACE

Now that you have a better idea how to recognize your people when you meet them and how to build a strong team around you, let's talk about finding your place in the world: the right seat on the bus, or the right spot in the wall, where you fit. After all, we are living stones, not dead bricks. Therefore, there is a divinely designed place in the wall where only you can fit.

One of the difficulties in becoming fully actualized occurs when you find yourself in a community that doesn't have the capacity or vision to collaborate with your calling. For example, if you want to be an actress, it might be good to move to Hollywood rather than stay in a community without the resources or opportunities to nurture an acting career. If you are called to be a singer, maybe Nashville is the place for you. New York is a great place to become a model, and Silicon Valley might be the best place for a high-tech start-up. But moving to Silicon Valley to pursue a career in modeling is probably a bad idea. Conversely, it might be tough to start a tech company in Hollywood. Although these examples are in no way absolutes, they serve to paint a picture of the collaboration that takes place when we discover our people *and* find our promised land, while also illustrating what happens when we try to fulfill our callings in the wrong community.

Am I saying that you could be in a community of people who have your DNA but still can't carry your vision? Yes! You could be with the right types of people but living in the wrong land, a place that can't support your mission.

Before you get frustrated or confused, let's look at an example of the way an environment helps to actualize a specific people group with a specific vision. In the book of Joshua when Joshua entered the promised land and defeated its inhabitants, he was instructed by God to distribute the land by tribe *and* by division. Each tribe of Israel was given a specific place by God (not just random acreage), which meant that each piece of land was given to a tribe, to a certain people group, and then to divisions within the tribe.

What might this look like for us? I like to think of the word *division* as di-vision or diverse-visions. The word *tribe* would refer to our people (as in finding the right people), and the word *di-vision* would be our missions in life (the roles we play amongst our people). We then need to find the place (our specific piece of the promised land) that will support our God-given missions.

Caleb's Hill Country

Joshua gave his good friend, Caleb, the first pick of the land. In Joshua 14:7, 10–12 Caleb said,

> I was forty years old when Moses the servant of the LORD sent me from Kadesh-barnea to spy out the land, and I brought word back to him as it was in my heart. . . . Now behold, the LORD has let me live, just as He spoke, these forty-five years, from the time that the LORD spoke this word to Moses, when Israel walked in the wilderness; and now behold, I am eighty-five years old today. I am still as strong today as I was in the day Moses sent me. . . . Now then, give me this hill country about which the LORD spoke on that day, for you heard on that day that [giant men called] Anakim were there, with great fortified cities; perhaps the LORD will be with me, and I will drive them out as the LORD has spoken.

I would like to point out that Caleb belonged to the tribe of Judah. Judah, as a tribe, was given a vast amount of land. The borders of their land are described in Joshua 15. Of that land, Caleb was given Hebron (the hill country). Not everyone in the tribe of Judah shared Caleb's vision, even though all of them had the same DNA. That's why the land had to be divided up by tribe *and* by division (di-vision). The tribe had enough flexibility to allow for diverse visions inside the same core perspectives and worldview.

Caleb's vision was to defeat the remaining giants in the

promised land; therefore, Joshua gave him the division of land that would fulfill his divine mission in life. Caleb received the land where the Anakim dwelled, the land of the giants!

The Right Land

Caleb was a warrior; therefore, he received land that was compatible with his vision. On the other hand, the sons of Reuben, the sons of Gad, and the sons of Manasseh had a large number of livestock. When they saw that the land of Jazer and the land of Gilead were great places for livestock, Gad and Reuben asked Moses for that land. (Moses had given these tribes their land before Joshua was put in charge). Moses didn't particularly like the idea because it was on the wilderness side of the river and was technically not the promised land. Eventually, Moses agreed to their request but insisted that they still cross the Jordan River and join forces with the rest of their brothers to help them conquer the promised land (Numbers 32). It's true that one man's promised land can somehow become another man's problem!

When shepherds are forced to cross over into the land best suited for warriors, their destinies are put at risk (unless you're King David, of course, who was a shepherd and a warrior) because people have very little grace for things they are not called to do and places that don't fit their destinies. How frustrating and unsuccessful following Caleb would have been for farmers who were forced to plant crops on the side of a mountain where the giants lived. They would never be satisfied because the land they were forced to occupy didn't support their vision.

If you are anything like me, you know many people who are much more successful in the Kingdom than yourself, and yet they don't put forth nearly the effort you do. I used to think these people were just a lot more gifted and talented than I am. Of course, this is true at times; but more often than not, they have simply found their sweet spot in life. They are warriors in a land of giants or shepherds in fertile grazing grounds. They are experiencing the synergistic and catalytic nature of the triune manifestation of the right people, with the same vision, in the perfect place.

Leaving Your Father's House

When you find yourself in the wrong place, despite being with the right people with the same vision, you must be willing to reevaluate whether God is calling you to a new, more fitting location or community. When Kathy and I left Weaverville we were both torn inside. We had spent twenty years in that small community building friendships and loving people. We had built a house in the woods and developed seven businesses in our town. We were woven into the fabric of every aspect of that city. Not only that, but Kathy and I were the senior leaders of Mountain Chapel, which really struggled when Bill and Beni left for Redding. We had installed Danny and Sheri Silk as the pastors of the church, but they were social workers who had never pastored a church before. Needless to say, their learning curve was pretty steep.

Kathy and I both wanted to be with Bill, but we also didn't want to leave our community of friends with whom we had grown so close. Then one day I realized that much like Abram and Sarai, who had to leave their country to follow God (Genesis 12), we had to let go of our community, our church, and our friends to fulfill our God-given destiny.

There are many reasons why you may choose to stay in "your father's house" instead of finding your promised land. Probably the most common reason is that you haven't yet found your people or your promised land, so you feel stuck. I certainly understand this. Kathy and I lived in San Jose, California, when we got married. We had great jobs, money in the bank, and a brand new house. More important, all of our family lived within thirty minutes of us. Outwardly we were living a dream, but inwardly we knew that we had to leave the place where we *grew up* to find the place we could *grow in* God. We didn't know where to go even though we knew where we couldn't stay.

If you are anything like Kathy and me, you might not know where you are headed, but you live with a deep longing for more. You know you can't stay where you are and still satisfy the intense passion within you. I would encourage you to consider following God with your whole heart and trusting Him to lead you. I find that there are times when the Lord is a "lamp to my feet" (Psalm 119:105). He only shows the next step. The main lesson in this season is to learn to trust Him with your destiny.

> SOMETIMES THE HOLY SPIRIT IS YOUR COMPASS, AND OTHER TIMES HE IS YOUR ROAD MAP.

Then there are other times when He is a "light to my path" (Psalm 119:105). I love it when the Lord shows me the path that reveals my destiny. Path revelations bring clarity and, conse-quently, meaning to the daily steps of life. So sometimes the Holy Spirit is your compass, and other times He is your road map. Whatever season you are in, He will guide you to your destiny and lead you into all truth.

Another reason why you might struggle with leaving could be that you feel obligated to stay in a church or a community, even though it's stifling you. It's common for people who love you to try to convince you to stay with them. Although most of them mean well, sometimes they use manipulation to try to stop you from going. Manipulation produces guilt (you owe us your life), shame (you have selfish motives for leaving), and fear (something terrible will happen if you go).

I don't want to be misunderstood here: I am not talking about walking away from your spouse and children in the name of following God! That's a perversion (the wrong version) of truth. Breaking up a family to "follow Jesus" is complete stupid-ity that only leads to pain and destruction. It bears no semblance to our Lord's covenant kingdom. I am referring to people outside of your immediate family who either refuse to move on in God or find themselves on a very different life journey than your own.

Leaving a community must be prayerfully and wisely con-sidered. Jesus was emphatic about not allowing your loyalties to people to undermine your covenant with Christ. I still cringe at the difficulty of His exhortation when He boldly proclaimed, "He who loves father or mother more than Me is not worthy of Me; and he who loves son or daughter more than Me is not wor-thy of Me. And he who does not take his cross and follow after Me is not worthy of Me" (Matthew 10:37–38).

I am inclined to explain away the sting of Jesus' words. Yet I am compelled to exhort you to embrace the pain (if indeed His words are painful to you), examine your journey, and boldly go where the Lord is leading you.

8

You're Standing on My Toes

When I was a boy I used to pretend I owned a helicopter. I would fly to the poorest places in the world and feed deprived people from its doors. My little sister and her stuffed animals were charged with pretending to be the needy, broken people who were starving. I, of course, was always the superhero who landed in the middle of the jungle just in time to rescue them!

As I grew older, my desire to help people grew stronger and more mature. I often found myself picking up hitchhikers and taking them home to feed them. I married young, and together my wife and I continued to reach out to the broken from our tiny house. Consequently, hurting people lived with us for seventeen of our first twenty years of marriage. In fact, I don't remember any of our children ever having his or her own bedroom.

My love for the broken has caused me to struggle over the years with pastors who seem untouchable, unreachable, or unavailable. So when I joined the Bethel Church team, I refused to have an unlisted phone number.

One night after work, Kathy and I went out for dinner. We arrived back home at 8:00 p.m., and I noticed our answering machine was beeping (anybody remember the days before cell phones?). I pushed the play button on the machine and was shocked by what I heard. There were thirty-eight messages from thirty different people on the tape, and they were *all* begging for help. Counseling was one of my primary responsibilities at the church, and I averaged six to eight sessions a day, four days a week; but I never expected this!

For several minutes the two of us endured the cries of desperation until finally Kathy couldn't take it any longer. With tears in her eyes she declared, "You have to help these people!"

Exhausted from a tough week of counseling, I shouted back, "You help them! I am maxed out! You have no idea how drained I am. I am done helping people. Needy people are everywhere. They are a bottomless pit, and they are killing me!"

The argument continued through the night as the two of us tried to come to terms with our situation. In fairness to Kathy, she had never seen me "peopled out." There was always enough love to go around in our home, and we helped almost everyone who asked for it. So Kathy was understandably upset when I refused to spend the night calling back thirty frantic people.

Over the next several months the challenge escalated. I tried to increase my counseling load to solve the problem, but every time I counseled one person, several more people would be sent to me for help. Sunday was the worst day of the week! After every service fifty people would gather at my seat for "prayer." I often dragged my butt to bed at one o'clock in the morning.

I was drowning in the sea of love. I wanted to run away and never come back. I finally got an unlisted phone number, but people just found other ways to get to me. I would lie in bed at night thinking of *all* the hurting people I had avoided during the day. Accusations flooded my mind. *You are a Pharisee. Remember the good Samaritan? He helped the person he encountered. But the Pharisee crossed the street to avoid the broken man's pain. You are doing the same thing your fathers the Pharisees did. If you cared about people, you would lay down your life for them. You just love the attention you get when you preach; you don't really love people. You are a whitewashed tomb full of dead men's bones . . . the bones of those you refused to help this week!*

To make matters worse, people I didn't have time to support wrote me terrible letters that helped to validate these indictments against my soul.

One night in desperation I prayed, "What do You want me to do with *all* of these hurting people?"

The Lord responded, "There is always enough time to help all the people I send to you. Furthermore, you only have answers for the people I send to you. So your job is to please Me and not to worry about what others think of you. You will always have the poor with you!"

A few months later, Jesus reprimanded me again. "You seem to have forgotten that I am the Savior of the world. You, on the other hand, are a laborer in the field. You just concern yourself with the task I have assigned you in the field I placed you in. In the meantime, I will remain the Redeemer of the planet."

It's been nearly twenty years since I listened to those desperate cries on my antiquated answering machine. To this day, I have not once laid my head on my pillow having personally met more than about 20 percent of the needs I am confronted with on any given day. There are seven billion people on this ailing planet, so I am convinced that the only people who meet the needs of everyone who asks for help live in insolation, or they lead self-absorbed lives.

Over these past few years I learned first how to survive and then, sometime later, how to thrive in the midst of this intense chaos. I finally came to grips with the fact that there's more to do in a day than any one of us can accomplish. Working harder may be necessary at times, but it won't ever solve the ultimate problem. The truth is if you become a provider of hope, you won't have to worry about the competition, because there will always be more customers than carriers.

Life is a delicate balance, a dance with time and priorities, a Holy Spirit journey of discovering what it means to be about our Father's business. In this crazy and chaotic world of intense need, we can only thrive when guided by Someone more brilliant than us.

Build Boundaries

Let me ask you a question: Is it common for you to rush from fire to fire feeling obligated to meet the needs of everyone who calls upon you? If you answered yes, then consider this: When you live that way, you leave the important people and divine purposes (that may not be on fire) neglected, deserted, and ignored. But the dysfunctional cycle doesn't stop there, because eventually the neglected essential people and your abandoned vital purposes catch on fire. Sometimes they are completely destroyed before you can free yourself from the obligations of others to douse the flames of distraction on your own divine connections and sovereign destiny.

Let me ask you a few more questions. Who initiates most of your meetings? Do you, or does someone else? Do you spend most of your days returning phone calls, or are you the one originating them? If you don't have a plan for your life, other people will provide one for you. The fact is, most of the needy people and many of the powerful people around you have strong opinions about what they think you should be doing.

You must set boundaries. When you don't set limits with people, they dictate your destiny, and your life becomes a menagerie of meeting other people's expectations while missing the call of God on your own life. God has given you a race to run, a fight to finish, and a path to follow. Don't let others distract you from it.

Great leaders must master the art of being deeply compassionate without letting the desires of others dictate their destinies or dominate their daily priorities. Let me be clear: I'm not talking about being self-centered or self-absorbed. Neither am I saying that the needs of others shouldn't influence your activities. They should!

In fact, in the middle of writing this chapter today, one of my team member's wives passed away. She was just forty-three years old with three young, beautiful children and the most amazing husband I have ever met. Yesterday I sat and wept with her. Her ten-year-old son sat by my side because he was convinced that if the two of us prayed for his mama (just one more time) she would be healed. Instead, twelve hours later she went home to be with the Lord.

I don't care how busy you are; you should never be too busy to touch the desperate needs of the people in your inner circle. This wasn't a disruption in my schedule; touching those who serve me and are in my family is part of my journey in the Spirit.

> YOU AND I ARE CALLED TO SERVE GOD BY SERVING PEOPLE. BUT WE ARE NOT CALLED TO SERVE PEOPLE INSTEAD OF SERVING GOD.

I hope you understand by now that I am not untouchable, rigid, or heartless; but I have decided that I will not fear people, nor will I be enslaved to them. You and I are called to serve God by serving people. But we are not called to serve people instead of serving God (Acts 5:29).

Being Misunderstood

One of the difficulties of pursuing the call of Jesus on your life is confronting the fear of man. If you fear people, you are not leading them; they are leading you. You must come to grips with the fact that if you are following Jesus and you refuse to fear people, you will be misunderstood. In the midst of that, remember that you are called to serve somebody, not called to touch everybody. The challenge is that many of the people you are not called to serve will disagree with you. What you do with the accusations of those people determines how much God can entrust to you.

One way that you can deal with being misunderstood is to harden your heart. I call it the "I don't care what you think" syndrome. But becoming hard-hearted and uncompassionate to protect your soul is a bad plan. You will wind up being just a shell of your destiny, and you will sabotage your ultimate purpose in life. It is therefore incumbent upon you to learn how to deal with false accusations, ridiculous expectations, desperate manipulation, and people's distorted perspectives of you.

I know what I am talking about. I have 220,000 followers on Facebook as of this writing, and it's growing at a rate of almost two thousand people a week. Unlike most leaders, I actually enjoy managing my own page. I get about twenty to fifty private messages a day on Facebook alone. Every day several people make huge requests of me, such as, "Can I make a counseling appointment with you?" "Here are five questions I have for you." "Can you call my mother and wish her a happy birthday?" "Can you give me a prophetic word?" "Here is my complex marriage problem. Can you tell me what I should do?"

Of course there is no way I can do any of these things and still have time to breathe, so I must graciously decline their requests. Sometimes their reactions can be shocking! Recently a young lady said I was treating her like a "[expletive] dog" and that I shouldn't even call myself a Christian. Why, you ask? Because I refused to set up a counseling appointment with her. (She is a

Facebook fan . . . we have never met.) I am not sure what people think leaders do all day, but evidently it's not much!

I work hard to remind myself that desperate times call for desperate measures, and when any of us are hurting we will do whatever it takes to get help. That is why I proactively recall the times I was so dang desperate that I violated every boundary to get help.

I recall one time when my eight-year-old daughter, Jaime, had a grand mal seizure at school. For some reason the school called me instead of an ambulance. Jaime had never had a seizure before, and I had never witnessed a seizure. I thought Jaime was dying! So I grabbed her, threw her in the passenger seat of our car, and raced to our doctor's office, ignoring every stop sign and speed limit. When I got there, I started yelling, "My daughter's dying! My daughter's dying! Where is Doctor Nielson?"

The nurses tried to calm me down, but I pushed them away as I ran from room to room shouting the doctor's name. When I barged into the last patient room, still trying to scream the doctor's name while completely out of breath, there was Doctor Nielson staring at me with a shocked expression on his face. He was performing a minor surgery on a patient when I forced my way into the room with three nurses in tow. Ignoring his plea to calm down, I grabbed him by the arm and forced him to my car, yelling, "She is dying, she is dying!" When we got to the car, Jaime was still in a full-blown seizure.

He looked up at me and said, "She isn't dying! She is having a seizure. She is going to be okay." Thankfully, after a year of many more seizures, several brain scans, and hospital stays, God healed

Jaime completely. It's been thirty years since that desperate day, and she has not had one seizure since she was healed.

Why did I tell you this story? Because we must remember how it feels to be desperate, so we can extend mercy to the people who violate our healthy boundaries in an effort to rescue themselves or their loved ones from trouble. Frankly, I often recall this painful story whenever someone does something crazy to get my attention.

When Jesus walked the earth people did radical things to get His attention. Desperate people ripped the roof off a house and lowered their friend down right in front of Jesus so He would heal him (Luke 5:18–20). Others screamed bloody murder to get His attention as He passed by (Mark 10:46–52). A sinful woman crashed a high-level dinner party to wash His feet with her tears and hair and expensive perfume (Luke 7:36–39). They were all frantic people who were starving for the Master's touch.

The world is filled with desperate, hurting, and dying people who will do anything to get help. You are called to help some of them, but if you don't learn how to say no and set healthy boundaries, soon you won't be able to help any of them. I could tell you a thousand stories of people who were offended by me, not because I did something wrong, but because I didn't have time to do anything for them. When these people reacted unhealthily, I could have chosen to build a wall around my heart to protect myself; instead, I have chosen to work hard at learning not to take their words to heart. I just try to focus on the mission God has called me to accomplish for Him and live in His peace.

I Am the Savior of the World . . . NOT!

In 2008 I found myself almost unable to get off my couch for six months. For the first time in my life I was fighting depression that was so deep it felt as if someone had dropped me in a dark hole in the earth and left me for dead. I seriously didn't want to live anymore. To make matters worse, I was having fifty panic attacks a day, and I didn't sleep for nearly six months.

It all started when one of my daughters had an emotional breakdown and couldn't leave her bedroom. With two small children who were crushed by her behavior, a husband who called me several times a day for help, and a church they pastored that was trying to understand their dilemma, it was unbelievably stressful.

That same month, Bill suddenly became deathly ill with Hepatitis C and was quarantined to his house. Danny Silk and I picked up most of Bill's conferences, along with our own. Consequently, we were traversing the earth to cover all of the bases.

Just as things started to improve slightly, my son walked into my office one day and told me that his marriage was in trouble. Eight months later, his wife ran away with a guy who got her pregnant, leaving three children and a broken husband to grieve!

I decided that it was my responsibility to fix all of this, so I became the savior of the world. But six months into my savior role I crashed and burned. I became another family casualty, an immobile tank burning on the side of the road overlooking a city on fire. It would take nearly three years for my family to recover. The complete story is in my book *Spirit Wars*, but it should suffice to say that I learned a few things about boundaries and not diverging from Jesus' calling during battle.

Let me close this chapter by stating the obvious: everyone has limits! I don't care who you are; if you don't set boundaries with people, they will work you to death and then say nice things about you at your funeral. I like the saying, "A man of too many friends comes to ruin" (Proverbs 18:24).

There are people all around you who love you; but the truth is, you are the only one on this earth who really knows you . . . your energy, your stress level, your fears, and your passions. No one else can set boundaries for you. You have to muster the courage to say no, to risk being misunderstood, to refuse to live under the expectations of others, to be satisfied at times with pleasing only God.

> YOU HAVE TO MUSTER THE COURAGE TO SAY NO, TO RISK BEING MISUNDERSTOOD, TO REFUSE TO LIVE UNDER THE EXPECTATIONS OF OTHERS, TO BE SATISFIED AT TIMES WITH PLEASING ONLY GOD.

This is the cross you must bear for the sake of your soul, for the sake of your family, and for the sake of the Kingdom. Boldly do what you have never done before, so you can be the person you have always wanted to be.

9

Forged in the Furnace

In the early '80s Kathy and I owned an auto parts store, and we (mostly I) decided to expand our business into two other cities. My decision had a deleterious effect on our cash flow to the point that we barely had money to feed our family. Our three children were young at the time, and we had strong convictions that they needed a full-time mom at home. This made it impossible for Kathy to work outside of the house to help pay our bills, so she set up her desk in our home and did all of our accounting and finance oversight, while simultaneously taking care of our small children. This was no easy task, but we worked hard and kept growing.

Kathy developed into a great chief financial officer for our four businesses in three locations with forty employees. Yet the faster we grew, the tighter things became financially, especially at home. I felt as if I was carrying the world on my shoulders. Growing a business from scratch can be agonizing, but developing three businesses all at the same time is like a mother having triplets . . . it will leave stretch marks on you for life. You might forget the pain you were in, but you never forget the intensity of the labor it took to give birth to your dreams.

It takes sacrifice to give birth to anything worthwhile. I remember coming home a little early one night in the midst of one of our toughest seasons. It was wintertime, so it was freezing cold and pitch-dark outside. I navigated our steep, snow-covered gravel driveway in our old, faded-green International Scout. When I finally reached the top of the driveway, I peered up at our small chalet and was bewildered that the lights were all off inside the house. At first I thought my family was gone, until I eyed Kathy's car covered in snow in our driveway. Adrenaline surged through my body as negative scenarios raced through my mind.

I slid to a stop on our icy driveway, jammed on the parking brake, and ran up the stairs to the deck. I was terrified of what I might see inside. My heart pounded out of my chest as I apprehensively turned the knob and opened the front door. When I breached the doorway, I eyed our wood stove on the wall opposite me. It was glowing red, the fire crackling within. The smell of burning wood filled the room. The rest of the house was completely dark, except for two lanterns that dimly lit the living room just in front of me. The furniture was pushed to the walls, and three little tents made out of blankets occupied the room.

With my heart still pounding, I yelled, "Is anybody home?"

Suddenly, three little people stuck their heads out of their makeshift tents and yelled, "Hi, Daddy!"

Surprised, I asked, "What are you kids doing?"

"We are camping!" they proclaimed, laughing in unison.

Just then Kathy rushed into the living room looking alarmed. "What are you doing home so early?" she asked, making her way through the maze of tents and out the front door.

She seemed sort of stressed, so I followed her outside, questioning her along the way. "What are you doing?"

A second later she was staring at the electrical panel on the side of the house. "I am turning on the electricity," she said nervously.

Without looking up she flipped on the main breaker, and the lights suddenly came to life.

"What the heck are you doing?" I demanded.

"I am doing what I can to help our family through this lean time," she responded, obviously trying not to make me feel bad. Kathy had budgeted our electric bill by determining how many kilowatts we could use every month. During the day, she would shut the main breaker off to stay within her budget, and then she would turn it back on before I got home so I wouldn't have to live in a dark house.

Our kids weren't upset that there was no money, because their mother made a game out of our challenge. To this day all three of my children are very resourceful with money. They didn't learn that from their father; they learned it by watching their mother from the flaps of their little tents as she brought strength to a very tough situation.

Not only did our children learn how to be resourceful, but their mother also taught them how to find joy in hard situations, how to live with a positive attitude all the time, and how to work hard for the things we wanted. She continues to demonstrate perseverance to our children and refuses to complain no matter our circumstances.

In the face of overwhelming odds, Kathy simply doesn't give up. Consequently, she has become our lighthouse in the midst of storms, the pillar we can hold onto in the strongest winds, and the voice of reason when we are afraid.

The Process of the Potter's Wheel

Kathy's attitude is foreign to most of us today. Society longs for a trouble-free life, a magic pill, a euphoric marriage, and the state of constant ecstasy. Many people dream of a perfect world, where perfect people live out a perfect life. But the truth is that between the promise of your destiny and the palace of your dreams is the process of the potter's wheel. It is on this wheel that you are fashioned for your destiny and formed for your future.

> BETWEEN THE PROMISE OF YOUR DESTINY AND THE PALACE OF YOUR DREAMS IS THE PROCESS OF THE POTTER'S WHEEL.

One reason some refuse to submit themselves to the potter's wheel is that they worship fun. Many people spend their entire fortunes trying to have fun, in hopes that pleasure will bring them some great sense of fulfillment. In fact, many believers have confused joy with fun. It may be because we often teach about joy and fun as if the words were synonymous. Nothing could be further from the truth!

For example, when the apostle James said, "Consider it all joy . . . when you encounter various trials" (James 1:2), he wasn't saying that trials are fun. He was simply reminding us that our outward circumstances should not dictate our inward attitudes. There certainly is nothing wrong with having fun—in fact, I prefer it—but when we make pleasure the *goal* of our lives, instead of the *fruit* of some of our activities, we miss out on the joy of sacrifice and the harvest of passion.

A Spirit-led life isn't always fun, but it is always filled with joy. The obsession people today have with pleasure has destroyed many marriages, devastated countless children, and undermined the purposes of God, probably more than any other single addiction. It is often the root cause of divorce, drug addiction, alcohol abuse, gambling, pornography, sex trafficking, and every kind of evil.

The truth is, when we walk with God there are times of pleasure during a life of pure, inherited joy, but it wasn't free! I am deeply concerned that those who inherited a blessed life through Christ have lost sight of its high cost. I don't doubt our victory, nor do I question our high calling, but I wonder at the lack of resolve that some believers have to engage society at the level of their greatest pain. I grieve over a gospel that is cloaked in benefits but requires no responsibility. We need to carve out a path through the snake-infested jungles of life and carry the weak back to a place of safety, rather than bask in His victory while many nations continue to live in oppression, poverty, and despair.

We are God's champions! We weren't called to sit around the palace sipping suds and polishing our armor. Nor were we called to hold a spiritual, body-of-Christ building contest, competing for the congregation's applause while the world goes to hell. We have been left behind to transform the world.

When Jesus said He was finished, He didn't say you were! In fact, when Paul spoke of his apostolic credentials, he unleashed a list of beatings that would have scared Arnold Schwarzenegger. The very man who taught us about great grace was entrenched in a battle that scarred his body and troubled his soul. Yet some believers are convinced that life in the Kingdom is like tiptoeing through the tulips. They think they will win the nations through some pool party or beauty pageant.

But women and men of radical faith and outrageous courage are forged in the fire of circumstances! They don't shrink back when things get hard; instead, they press in and increase their intensity. When they see the naive stumbling through darkness, they rise with wisdom to rescue helpless souls.

Champions refuse to be moved by the crowd or intimidated by fear. Their loyalty can't be purchased, and their souls are not for sale. They have dared to leave the cesspool of unrighteous living to embrace a life of dignity and nobility.

OVERWHELMED

Even if you walk with radical faith and outrageous courage, you sometimes go through seasons when the mere frequency of things going wrong in your life can be discouraging and overwhelming. One of the worst things that can happen in these seasons is that you begin to *expect* things to go wrong. Expectation is the fruit of faith. In other words, you *believe* things are going to go wrong, and therefore you empower destructive outcomes. Simply put, by faith, your life sucks!

Of course, all of us have been surprised when something unexpected went wrong in our lives, but it's important that you don't turn bad circumstances into a lifetime of cynicism, and subsequently invite a foreboding spirit into your life. *Foreboding* means, "an impending sense of doom." It's the feeling that something is always about to go wrong. If you're having a good day, you fear a bad day is coming. Once this spirit grips your soul, you always prepare for the worst so you won't be disappointed. You usually aren't disappointed, because you believed and therefore received a negative outcome.

I have watched this negative ecosystem play out in so many people's lives. For example, years ago I had a woman working for me (I will call her Mary) who was in a car accident. She was sitting at a stoplight, minding her own business, when a drunk driver plowed into the back of her car. It destroyed her automobile and gave her a terrible case of whiplash. For nearly two years she suffered with severe back pain and migraine headaches. But the worst thing was that Mary began to fear that she would get in another accident. Her fear was extenuated by the fact that she was a victim in the first car accident. This caused Mary to feel powerless to avoid another accident because she didn't do anything to cause the first one.

A couple of years passed, and just as Mary was starting to feel normal, she got hit again at a stoplight. Not only did the crash reinjure her back, but it also intensified her fear of accidents. Mary worked for me for five more years, and in that short time she was involved in four more auto accidents. Do you know what the craziest thing about this was? Not one of those accidents was her fault! I don't mean that Mary blamed her bad driving habits on other people; I am saying that *none* of her six auto accidents had anything to do with her driving. Yet Mary's fear of another accident caused her to believe that she would crash again. Fear is actually faith in the wrong kingdom. Since she lived by faith, she empowered the kingdom of darkness to torment her. I am convinced that this is how people jinx themselves. Yet Jesus died to break the curse over our souls and give us abundant lives!

I am not saying that we need to be optimists rather than pessimists, but that we need to be believers. Both optimists and believers manifest positive attitudes, but for very different reasons. An optimist sees the glass half-full, but a believer knows it's not the level of the water in the glass that matters as much as whether or not it's being filled or depleted. Therefore it's the capacity of the resource that determines the condition of life's circumstances.

When you walk by faith, you tap into the artesian well of unlimited resources. Believing in Jesus is not a preconditioned mental attitude toward life's circumstances but the acknowledgment that your temporal conditions are subject to His supernatural power. Therefore, truth overrides the facts because the facts are rooted in the natural laws of creation, while truth is always rooted in the transcending power of the Spirit, which is accessed through faith.

Here are nine keys to breaking the negative ecosystem in your life and embracing faith:

Look for Jesus in the midst of your troubles. He tends to hang out in hard places.

Meditate on God's past miracles and works in your life, not on your tragedy.

Cultivate thankfulness in your heart no matter how you feel. You don't have to give thanks *for* everything, but know who you are and whose you are. Then you can give thanks *in* everything.

Avoid the misery-loves-company syndrome by disciplining yourself to hang around happy people, even when you don't feel like it.

Pray in the Spirit, because you are "building yourselves up" when you do (Jude 20).

Take a mental vacation every day. Give yourself permission to take a break from thinking about life's challenges, and cultivate some happy thoughts.

Remind yourself that these circumstances will not last forever. The Bible frequently says, "It came to pass." In other words, it came so it could pass . . . this season will end.

Don't forget that everything works out for good in the end. So if it isn't good, then it isn't the end (Romans 8:28).

Refuse to partner with any thought that doesn't inspire hope because any thought that doesn't inspire hope is rooted in a lie. You have the mind of Christ, so don't allow any thought in your mind that isn't in His.

These are not quick fixes but ways to process life so that you don't let go of God's promises in the midst of your problems.

TAKE IT FROM ROCKY

I enjoy movies that embody the struggle of the human soul for greatness. I think Sylvester Stallone captured this struggle well in *Rocky Balboa*. It is currently the penultimate movie in the *Rocky* film franchise, and it has some of the best dialogue ever scripted.

The plot centers on an aged Rocky who wants to make a comeback. Through a series of events, the current boxing champion challenges Rocky to a ten-round exhibition match, but Rocky must first convince the boxing federation to license him to fight again. Rocky's greatest test turns out to be his son, Robert, who sees his father as a has-been who needs to hang up his gloves and fade into obscurity.

As the camera focuses in on their passionate argument in a Philadelphia back alley, the real issue emerges: Robert begins yelling about living in the shadow of his father's fame. As Robert turns to walk away, Rocky calls him back and begins to tell him about his childhood:

> I'd hold you up to say to your mother, "This kid's gonna be the best kid in the world. This kid's gonna be somebody better than anybody I ever knew." And you grew up good and wonderful. It was great just watching you; every day was like a privilege. Then the time come for you to be your own man and take on the world, and you did. But somewhere along the line, you changed. You stopped being you. You let people stick a finger in your face and tell you you're no good. And when things got hard, you started looking for something to blame, like a big shadow.
>
> Let me tell you something you already know. The world

ain't all sunshine and rainbows. It's a very mean and nasty place, and I don't care how tough you are. It will beat you to your knees and keep you there permanently if you let it. You, me, or nobody is gonna hit as hard as life. But it ain't about how hard ya hit. It's about how hard you can get hit and keep moving forward. How much you can take and keep moving forward. That's how winning is done! Now if you know what you're worth, then go out and get what you're worth. But ya gotta be willing to take the hits, and not pointing fingers saying you ain't where you wanna be because of him, or her, or anybody! Cowards do that, and that ain't you! You're better than that! I'm always gonna love you no matter what. No matter what happens. You're my son, and you're my blood. You're the best thing in my life. But until you start believing in yourself, ya ain't gonna have a life![1]

I can't think of a better way to close this chapter except to say that sometimes movies are realistic depictions of truth. And it's the truth that sets you free (John 8:32).

10

WALKING OUT OF PAIN

When Lazarus emerged from his tomb at the voice of the Master, he was *alive yet bound*. Jesus turned to the people near him and said, "Unbind him, and let him go" (John 11:44).

Too many of us are spiritual mummies; we've had true conversion experiences, but we live lives encumbered by the same things that entombed us in the first place. If we truly want to reach the heights of where God has called us to be, we need to discover how to remove the grave clothes that

> TOO MANY OF US ARE SPIRITUAL MUMMIES; WE'VE HAD TRUE CONVERSION EXPERIENCES, BUT WE LIVE LIVES ENCUMBERED BY THE SAME THINGS THAT ENTOMBED US IN THE FIRST PLACE.

relegate us to lives of repression and restrict us from achieving our full potentials.

Mummified Mentors

I lost my father when I was three years old, and subsequently, two very broken stepfathers raised me. Neither of them knew how to manage their own lives much less nurture a family. Consequently, I carried the scars of a broken heart and the wounds of rejection deep into my life with God. Although I had a powerful salvation experience when I was eighteen years old, the lens through which I viewed life was skewed. To make matters worse, I was unconsciously ignorant; I didn't know that I didn't know. I was deceived as to the level of my brokenness.

One of the greatest areas of deception in my life was my capacity to love myself. Jesus said, "to love your neighbor as you love yourself" (Matthew 22:39). I certainly was doing that. I didn't love myself, therefore I couldn't love anyone else. My predicament was complicated by my definition of humility, which was reinforced by the religious community that led me to Christ. Our culture taught us that it was prideful to feel great about ourselves. We believed true humility focused on our flaws, our weaknesses, and our brokenness. As far as we were concerned, the blood of Jesus was enough to forgive our sins, but it didn't have the power to transform us into new creations.

I was a mummy among mummies! My brothers and sisters couldn't unbind me because they were themselves tombless yet bound. Mummification was in vogue. The stench of self-abuse and self-sacrifice filled the atmosphere, which reinforced the idea that self-love was rooted in evil. The irony is that we were believers desperately wanting to be more like Christ, yet hating what He created. Our belief system was deeply rooted in deception. We thought that in order to be like Him, we had to embrace pain.

Many years have passed since I was a self-loathing Christian. I have learned a lot about the process of unbinding the Lazaruses of the world through my own experience of becoming free and living peacefully. One of the things I have learned is that most people are unconsciously ignorant, as I was. They have all the symptoms of a mummified life, but because they've never known freedom, they are unaware that there is a better way to live.

I think the old adage is true: if it looks like a duck, walks like a duck, and quacks like a duck; it's probably a duck! So let me lay out fifteen characteristics of people who are alive but bound:

1. They always feel like something's about to go wrong.
2. They live with a high level of anxiety most of the time.
3. They feel as if their thoughts control them; they don't control their thoughts.
4. They struggle with not trusting people.
5. Their relationships are superficial.
6. They secretly compete with people most of the time.
7. They wish they were somebody else.
8. They get their feelings hurt very easily.
9. They have a hard time sleeping.
10. When people compliment them, they can't accept the praise.

11. They are easily intimidated by others and have very little confidence in themselves.
12. They have unhealthy attractions to anyone who shows them attention.
13. They struggle with depression and destructive or suicidal thoughts.
14. They are hyperspiritual to the point of fantasy.
15. They often feel as if God is mad at them.

This is not the last word on mummified symptoms. I just want to get you thinking about your own life in a way that can move you from being unconsciously ignorant to consciously informed.

The fact that you have struggled with one or more of these symptoms in a few seasons of your life doesn't necessarily mean you are still bound. You would be hard-pressed to find any human being who has never dealt with these unhealthy symptoms at some point in his or her life. On the other hand, if any of these or other destructive characteristics describe you today, then it would greatly benefit you to embrace the process of unbinding.

Let's start by taking a look at the journey from pain to freedom.

Confront the Pain

Marion was a stunningly beautiful young lady. She had long blonde hair, deep-blue eyes, and a face that belonged on the cover of a magazine. This woman carried herself like royalty and seemed to have everything going for her.

One day, Marion sat gracefully on the couch in my office recounting her story. Through her tears she began to explain how desperately she wanted to be married but had yet to find love. At thirty-two years old, Marion had dated many guys through the years, and she was even engaged twice. However, every time the relationship became serious, Marion would suddenly discover that "the guy wasn't right for her." After fourteen years of yearning to be married, she was desperate for some outside counsel.

I listened intently to her story for nearly an hour. After a while, I began to see a pattern emerge from the hologram of her life. In each case the names of her boyfriends changed, but the story remained the same. Finally I interrupted her and asked a seemingly unrelated question.

"Marion, what are you afraid of?" I asked abruptly.

She looked stunned. "What do you mean?" she asked defensively.

"I mean, every time you become intimate (not sexually) with a guy, you discover flaws in his character and ultimately blow up your relationship with him." I continued, "Marion, love covers a multitude of sins, but fear transforms the gift of discernment into suspicion. Suspicion is the wicked stepsister of discernment; it's a faultfinding, critical spirit that masquerades as caring, but it's really out to destroy your relationships."

I could feel the tension rising in the room as Marion contemplated my probing question. Speechless, she shook her head and mouthed the words, "I don't know." Tears streamed from her eyes as if she had opened a closet in her mind, only to find more brokenness.

I continued to probe for another hour; deeper and deeper I

dove into her soul, peeling off fears like the layers of an onion. When we finally worked our way through all of the layers of fear, at the center was a terribly common problem. So common, in fact, I am surprised I didn't catch it the moment she sat down.

Marion adored her father, but when she was ten years old, he left her mother for another woman. The divorce broke the bond between this dad and his little girl and subsequently smashed her heart into tiny pieces. She had tried to recover over the years, but the scars on Marion's heart told her stories. They said, "There is something wrong with you. You aren't lovable, valuable, or beautiful."

Pushed by the incessant voices, Marion fought back by compulsively working out a couple of hours each day. However, she soon discovered that wasn't enough. Her desperate need to be adored intensified, and so did her rash decisions. Marion quickly found herself heading down the destructive road of self-hatred. Cosmetic surgery and breast implants only numbed the pain momentarily, and it wasn't long before her scars imprisoned her.

Marion's desperation had nothing to do with finding the right guy; in fact, she was terrified of intimacy. Whenever her boyfriends got close enough to see into her heart, she would build a case against them and reject them before they had a chance to reject her. She couldn't stand the thought of letting them see her scars and dump her the way her father had. The crazy thing was that Marion had felt the pain but never connected the dots in her mind.

Marion's pain was finally greater than her fear of being rejected. Ultimately, this resulted in her facing her fear and defeating her giant.

It's nearly impossible to change our realities until we have questioned them. But we can't question what we refuse to confront.

Jesus said, "Blessed are those who mourn, for they shall be comforted" (Matthew 5:4). In other words, mourning is necessary; it's the process that leads to wholeness. Yet many Christians are afraid of pain and believe their only responsibilities are to cheer people up. Consequently, hurting people push down their pain instead of confronting it, and they undermine the mourning process as Marion did. This leads to a life of unresolved agony. Their pain ferments in the unconscious closets of their souls and manifests in brokenness in their daily lives.

As children of God, we must learn how to walk away from pain (not hide it), so that we can become healthy and whole people who live joyful lives. With this in mind, I often ask congregations, "What is your process for dealing with pain, and what do you do with your pain?" Almost without exception I hear something to the effect of, "I just give it to the Lord," or "I lay it at the foot of the cross." This sounds biblically beautiful, but when I ask them how they practically lay their pain at the foot of the cross, 90 percent of the time someone says, "I'm not sure." So let's take a look at some practical steps for walking away from pain.

1. *Forgive those who caused you pain.* Forgiveness is the first step on your journey out of the pain. To illustrate this, Jesus told a story about a slave who owed a king a ton of money. The king graciously forgave the slave, but that same slave refused to forgive the debt of his fellow slave who owed him a small sum of money. Instead, he had him thrown into prison! When the king heard of it, he

said to the merciless slave, "'Should you not also have had mercy on your fellow slave, in the same way that I had mercy on you?' In anger his master handed him over to the jailers to be tortured, until he should pay back all he owed" (Matthew 18:33–34).

Unforgiveness opens the door for tormentors to harass you, ultimately perpetuating and increasing your pain. But forgiveness shuts out bondage and frees you to begin living in peace.

There are a few things that you should know about forgiveness. First of all, forgiveness is an act of your will, not a manifestation of your desire. In other words, forgiveness doesn't have to feel good. It's also not the last step in your journey out of pain. For example, if you lend someone $10,000 and she doesn't pay you back, forgiving her means you no longer send her a bill because you have erased the debt. It doesn't mean when money is tight that you don't wish you had your $10,000 back. Therefore, forgiveness is not an emotional decision but a willful act.

Second, forgiving someone doesn't preclude you from experiencing pain when he or she is around. Having negative feelings about a person doesn't mean you didn't forgive him or her. Forgiveness simply means you no longer *will* the person to be punished. Let's say I ran over you on purpose and broke both your legs. Forgiving me will have no practical effect on the level of pain that you experience in your body. Forgiveness frees you from the tormentors, but it doesn't necessarily heal all the pain others have caused in your life.

Finally, forgiving someone doesn't mean you trust him. Let's imagine that a person is raped in a dark alley. That victim needs to forgive the rapist so the tormentors leave her alone, but she should never trust the rapist.

2. *Change the way you think about pain.* One of the greatest misconceptions people have about pain is that time heals. They believe that if they just forget about it, ignore what they're feeling, or overlook what's happened to them, then their pain will eventually go away. This couldn't be further from the truth! If time healed, people in prison would be the most whole people in the world.

Time is a revealer and an enabler. If you plant a seed in the ground and water it, in time it will grow. The same thing happens with pain. When you hide pain deep in your soul and water it with bitterness and unforgiveness, in time these things become like weeds. They will grow up around your heart and choke out every semblance of happiness. In the same way, though, if you go through the powerful process of facing your pain and proactively weeding your "heart garden," then in time you will be made whole.

The obvious challenge is that it's never fun. Hebrews 12:2 says, "For the joy set before [Jesus], He endured the cross"! Jesus was able to endure the pain of the cross (He didn't enjoy it) because He focused on what He was gaining, not on the price He was paying. Likewise, James says, "Consider it pure joy, my brothers and sisters, whenever you face trials of many kinds, because you know that the testing of your faith produces perseverance.

Let perseverance finish its work so that you may be
mature and complete, not lacking anything" (vv. 1:2–4
NIV). At first glance, this seems ridiculous! I mean, when
was the last time your world burst into flames and you
called your friends to rejoice that perseverance is finishing
its work and that soon you will be without lack? I'll
be the first to admit that this is usually not my initial
response.

Over the course of many trials and tribulations, I
have learned the value of finding joy in the process of my
pain and of looking forward to the outcome. Joy—or the
promise of joy—gives you the ability to face seemingly
impossible circumstances and helps you to thrive when
life is hard. It's critical that you change the way you think
about trials, pain, and perseverance, so that the joy of the
Lord will become your strength in the tough seasons of
your life.

Jesus and James both emphasized the *vision factor*:
the ability to perceive the outcome of the process while
you are still in the midst of it. Vision gives your pain a
purpose. It's important to understand that the apostle
James is talking about fighting *from* victory instead of
fighting *for* victory. Despite the trials that awaited him,
vision postured him to experience the outcome in the
midst of the process.

Many of us fall victim to the belief that we have
to claw and scratch our ways to victory. We become
professional survivors who cling to the foot of the cross
because we are terrified of the impending doom. We

grope in darkness, hoping only to be rescued. Yet when we face pain, embrace the process, and envision victory, we become impossible to defeat!

3. *Allow yourself to mourn.* Contrary to popular opinion, mourning isn't sitting in a dark room thinking about your agony until you become angry and overwhelmed. This may be a part of your process, but it certainly isn't the endgame. The process of mourning that leads to wholeness has a beginning and an end. As you would at a funeral, you experience grief as you recount the loss, yet tears tend to wash away your pain as you process your memories and recount your history.

In 2008 my son, Jason, went through the hardest season of his life. Through a series of events, he found himself in the middle of a divorce. After ten years of marriage and three kids, Jason was drowning in an ocean of pain, and there seemed to be no way out of it. His options dwindled as his world imploded, collapsing his heart in on itself. Every beautiful memory crumbled into a horrible nightmare.

Yet Jason chose to embrace the pain, look each memory in the face, and process it with honesty, grief, and truth. It was slow going and required patience, humility, and a yielding of his will as he invited God into his powerless places and followed Jesus out of the pit. He allowed the mourning process to run its course and lead him to wholeness.

4. *Examine your troubled thoughts.* Sometimes during the process of walking out of pain, you become so distressed

that your thoughts are like troubled children arguing with their siblings. The noise and confusion can be so dramatic that it is nearly impossible to concentrate on the voice of God. This often causes you to feel alone and afraid.

In seasons such as these, it is necessary to deal with each screaming thought individually. Separate your troubled thoughts and interview them independently, the way you would question quarreling children to uncover their offenses. This step is often the most challenging because it requires you to dig down to your root issues as you examine your anxious thoughts. But facing your pain head-on is the only way to find true resolve and, ultimately, closure.

Whether you are paralyzed with pain or just walking with a limp, this process will help you to exit your painful prison and live fully actualized.

5. *Strengthen your broken places.* After you have discovered your broken places and spent time interviewing your thoughts, the next step is to strengthen the weak places in your soul. For example, if you've spent your whole life shut down because you're afraid of being rejected and hurt, then I suggest you read a great book on boundaries. It also might be wise to listen to some teaching on how to communicate your feelings. Then, metaphorically speaking, you haven't just stopped your kids from arguing; you have taught them how to communicate. This is the way to become a powerful person in every area of life.

Let me give you another example. Let's say that you are afraid to cry or process your emotions. I would highly recommend getting a journal and spending time with God to process your past pain. Allow Him to answer questions that have carried hurt. You might even write letters to people who have hurt you, though it's best never to send the letters. This exercise would be for dealing with your own pain.

Regardless of the reasons you're hurting or you're numb, the way out is to dive in. By doing this, you will become a master at discovering your pain, communicating for closure, and healing your soul.

6. *Pace yourself through pain.* One of the most common questions people ask is, How often should I process my pain? Eventually you're going to need to work through every painful thought and memory, because anything you're afraid to examine is going to keep you bound. However, processing pain is a lot like lifting weights. If you lift weights every day, all day long, instead of getting stronger you'll break your body down to the point that it can't do anything. In the same way, if you process all day long, every day, you will have what we call an emotional breakdown. Therefore, it's essential that you pace yourself.

It's also important, as you are working through emotional times or stressful seasons, that you eat healthily, sleep well, exercise often, and have fun. I've found that most people who have breakdowns ignore these basic elements of healthy living.

If you find yourself slipping into depression or anxiety, it's most likely because you are either processing too quickly or you are believing a lie. Anytime you are close to feeling hopeless, slow down and refocus on God's perspective through your own relationship with Him and with the help of others. We were never meant to live in isolation. Take the time to build a community of friends who will remind you about your true identity and your divine destiny.

Be patient with yourself through this journey, and think of this season as a marathon rather than a sprint. The goal is for you to make progress little by little, every day. If you have three good days in a week and suddenly have three tough days, don't think of it as a setback. In fact, encourage yourself by reminding your soul that you are halfway there! Try to keep the big picture in mind while you are in the process of healing. You will have some hard days on the way to wholeness, but you will become a much stronger person in the end. Embrace the journey!

> REGARDLESS OF THE REASONS YOU'RE HURTING OR YOU'RE NUMB, THE WAY OUT IS TO DIVE IN.

11

SIDEWALKS TO SUCCESS

Several years ago, when Shasta College was being constructed in Redding, California, the contractor didn't install the sidewalks immediately after finishing the building. Instead, he planted the lawn around the entire campus and then waited a year to see where the people wore out the grass. When the year was over, the contractor poured sidewalks in the worn sections of the lawn so that the walkways followed the actual routes of the students and faculty.

We all need pathways—structures—that take into account our strengths, maximize our purposes, and cover our weaknesses. Yet many of us live with structures that were built for someone else or constructed for a different season in life, so they keep us from being fully actualized.

You might be asking how important it is to have a structure

designed specifically for you. Well, let me give you a great example of how structures can make or break you.

When America's forefathers drafted our Constitution, they were interested in creating a very different governmental structure than the British monarchy that once ruled them. They thought Britain's king had way too much power. In response, they created a constitutional republic to limit our president's authority and balance the decision-making power among three branches of government and the majority of our citizens.

But as our forefathers contemplated our young country's future, they realized that a republic is great in a time of peace; but if our nation were ever under siege, a structure with so many checks and balances would process decisions too slowly to win a war at home.

With this in mind, they provided something in the Constitution called *martial law*. When Congress enacts martial law, our government is transformed into a military structure. This empowers our president to make decisions necessary to win battles without the time constraints of the congressional approval required in peacetime. Even if the United States had the greatest military general in the history of the world as our president, without martial law the governmental structure itself would restrict his or her ability to lead our forces into victory.

It is clearly important to have the right structure in place for the right season. Is it possible that your current life's structure was built for a different season, that you have been struggling to reach your destiny simply because of an outdated way of doing things? Let's look at an antiquated structure that resisted a new epoch in history.

It was 1908 in America, and the first Model Ts had just begun to roll off the assembly line. The cars cost $825.00, and Henry Ford was selling them like hotcakes at a loggers' convention. Before the year was over, Ford had delivered ten thousand of these babies to people all over the country. Four short years later, Henry dropped the price to $575.00, and the sales soared yet again. But people were still arguing over which form of transportation was more efficient: cars or horses. The comparisons raged on, with Ford measuring the strength of their cars in "horsepower" . . . twenty horsepower to be exact.

But the real challenge facing Ford had nothing to do with the automobile itself. All the transportation structures in place had been developed around horses. Narrow, dirt roads had been built for horses instead of wide, paved highways constructed for cars. Stables were everywhere, but there were no gas stations. Farriers were in stables in every town, but there were no mechanics. Veterinarians took care of horses, but there were no repair shops. Even though automobiles were a much better form of transportation, it would be years before America realized the full potential of the car, simply because of the constraints of the infrastructure.

What does this mean for you? Maybe you're a Ferrari driving on a dirt trail hewed out for horses, wondering why you can't get any traction. If you're feeling stuck, it might be a good idea to consider whether the structures around you are conducive to what you're called to do.

For example, if you are working in a church as a songwriter and worship leader, then an 8:00 a.m. to 5:00 p.m. schedule is probably not the best structure for you, because inspiration refuses to be confined to a clock or calendar. You may be in the middle of writing a song, chasing the melody through a meadow in your mind, and then you realize that your shift is over. Yet, you know that you can't leave, because the vision is fading into obscurity. Therefore, you chase the melody all night and finally leave your post in the wee hours of the morning. But the schedule says that you must be back in your office by 8:00 a.m.!

Creative people need flexibility, so they can chase inspiration without the constraints of a schedule designed for factory workers on an assembly line. This is what we discovered with Bethel Media.

Bethel Media is an $8 million nonprofit business owned and operated by Bethel Church. We started the business fifteen years ago when we began copying Bill Johnson's sermons onto cassette tapes and selling them to people who wanted them. In the first year our tiny business lost $60,000. Eventually, we figured out that the business had to be moved out of the pastoral wing of the building because the atmosphere was designed around dialogue, not production.

We took over a modular building one hundred feet from the pastoral wing, and suddenly our profits soared. In fact, the second year we made $60,000 in profit! You might be asking, what created such a dramatic turnaround in such a short time? The answer is simple: we built a structure that emphasized and thus maximized productivity. In the pastoral wing, success was measured by lives changed through conversation and prayer. But Bethel Media changed lives through products that people could listen to and watch. The more cassette tapes we produced, the more people were helped by our ministry. Unlike Bethel Church,

Bethel Media's goal was not to build relationships with the world but to produce as many cassette tapes as possible each hour.

We found it impossible to keep people focused on production in a culture built for conversation. In other words, we had the right people, but they were in the wrong structure. The moral of the story is simple: if you want to maximize your full potential, you have to discover, develop, and deploy a structure that is pro-actively built for you.

Assessing Your Destiny

In my life journey, I have discovered five main questions to keep in mind when proactively creating structures built for success. Misunderstanding the answers to any of these will form structures that limit, resist, or even derail your destiny. The truth is, whatever you misdiagnose you will mistreat.

So let's take a closer look at these five foundational questions. The following lists are meant to help you process and proactively evaluate the structures with which you are currently living, so you can determine whether they are empower

WHATEVER YOU MISDIAGNOSE YOU WILL MISTREAT.

ing or constraining you. But these are not complete lists. They are catalysts to inspire you to catalog the qualities in you that need protection and that need empowerment in order for you to achieve your goals in life.

1. *Who is leading?* The apostle Paul said, "I say to everyone among you not to think more highly of himself than he ought to think; but to think so as to have sound judgment" (Romans 12:3). So the first step to determining what structure will maximize God's purposes through you is to look inward, and to do so with sound judgment. Here are some examples of questions that might reveal the characteristics you need to be aware of as you consider what structure best complements you and the calling God has on your life.

   - What are your greatest strengths?
   - What are your greatest weaknesses or constraints?
   - Are you an internal or external processor?
   - What is your greatest fear?
   - What is your greatest passion?
   - Are you a visionary or an administrator?
   - Are you introverted or extroverted?
   - Are you highly relational? Does interacting with people make you feel alive or overwhelmed, intimidated, and exhausted?
   - Are you transparent by nature or intensely private?
   - Are you good at facing people, or do you avoid confrontation?
   - How do you interact with people around you? Are you a teacher, parent, exhorter, inspirer, comforter, or protector?
   - Are you a leader or a manager? Are you a risk-taker who lives in the future and is passionate about reproducing the vision you have inside? Or are you

someone who values security and naturally creates safe environments where expectations are consistently met and trust is built?

2. *Who are the people you are leading?* My close friend, Paul Manwaring, is a great leader on our staff. He leads our Global Legacy churches and network. But before Paul came to Bethel Church, he was a prison governor for a juvenile facility in England. I am sure the contrast between the people he was leading and is now leading is obvious, but allow me to explain it further.

When Paul was in England, he led those whom society had to control from the outside because they refused to exercise self-control. Therefore, much of the leadership structure in the prison was based around control, rehabilitation, and cognizant retraining. Conversely, Global Legacy is a network of church leaders, who, for the most part, have excellent characters. They have gathered of their own free wills to be inspired, trained, and equipped to grow their churches and transform their cities.

Imagine what would have happened if Paul had established the same structure for his Global Legacy leaders as he used with his juvenile prisoners, or vice versa. Frankly, leaders make this mistake all the time. They take the structures that worked for them previously and superimpose them over their new leadership assignments. Then they wonder why they used to be so successful but aren't anymore.

To help you avoid this pitfall, here are some examples

of questions you should consider about the people you are called to lead:

- What are the greatest strengths of your people?
- What are your people's greatest weaknesses?
- Are your people mature or new believers?
- What is the social or economic dynamic of your people?
- What level of favor and respect do you have with your people? Do they trust you? If so, at what level and in what areas do they trust you?
- How do your people perceive themselves? Are their perceptions accurate?
- Metaphorically speaking, are your people civilians or soldiers?
- Are your people lovers or warriors?
- How do your people relate to money? Are they generous, frugal, cynical, and so on?
- Are your people leaders, thinkers, highly educated, politically minded, or followers?
- How do your people relate to you? Are they your family, friends, workers, slaves, etc.?
- How would your people see you? As their parent, leader, boss, friend, spiritual guru, or something else?
- Are your followers infants, children, teenagers, sons and daughters, fathers and mothers, or grandfathers and grandmothers?
- When people come into your organization, do they think it's a hospital, counseling center, army barracks, school, country club, family reunion, worship center, bomb shelter, or party?

- What are the spiritual, mental, and physical conditions of your followers? Are they tired, zealous, sick, healthy, wounded, fragile, strong, hopeless, hungry, overfed, or full of faith?

3. *In what season are you leading?* The Israelites living in exile in Babylon taught us that life happens in seasons. Read Ecclesiastes 3:1–8 introspectively, and consider what might be your current season:

> There is an appointed time for everything. And there is a time for every event under heaven—
>
> A time to give birth and a time to die;
> A time to plant and a time to uproot what is planted.
> A time to kill and a time to heal;
> A time to tear down and a time to build up.
> A time to weep and a time to laugh;
> A time to mourn and a time to dance.
> A time to throw stones and a time to gather stones;
> A time to embrace and a time to shun embracing.
> A time to search and a time to give up as lost;
> A time to keep and a time to throw away.
> A time to tear apart and a time to sew together;
> A time to be silent and a time to speak.
> A time to love and a time to hate;
> A time for war and a time for peace.

You must build structures that are relevant to the season in which you find yourself, so let me ask the same question about seasons in a different way. What time is it?

Can you imagine trying to plant corn in the dead of winter, build a house in the midst of a war, or insist that your two-year-old son or daughter learn calculus? These examples seem ridiculous, but leaders do this type of mismatching all the time.

It's imperative that you understand the season you and your people are in, so you can build structures that are congruent with the times. Otherwise you might find yourself trying to snow ski in the middle of the summer.

Asking yourself the right questions about timing is key to building great roads to your destination, so it would be wise to consider these kinds of questions for every sphere you lead. In other words, if your family is in one season and your business is in another, then two completely different structures are required.

Here some questions to get you started, but you would be wise to develop your own questions that are relevant to you and the organization you are leading.

- Is it a time of war or a time of peace?
- Is it winter or harvest time?
- If your group were a house, would it be time to lay a foundation, install the roof, or decorate the house?
- Is it time to tear down or a time to build?
- Where is this organization in its life cycle: a start-up, growing, mature, in decline, or starting over?
- Metaphorically speaking, is it time to rest by the still waters, walk through the valley of the shadow of death, or celebrate your victories?
- If this organization were a person, where would he

or she be in life: having children, raising teenagers, marrying off sons and daughters, writing a will, or transitioning to the succession plan?

4. *What are you called to accomplish in this season?* As you are determining what your calling is during this time and what structures would support it, remember all we've considered thus far including who you are as a leader, who it is specifically that you are leading (and their levels of experience and capability), and in what season you are leading them. You must also consider your organization or community as a whole.

Here are some examples of questions regarding what you are called to accomplish. Again, I encourage you to come up with your own questions that fit you and the organizations you are leading.

- What is the mission (the *why*) of your organization?
- What is the vision (the *what*) of your organization?
- What are the plans (the *how*) for your organization to fulfill its mission and see its vision accomplished?
- What are the goals (the *when*) of your organization? List specific accomplishments with timelines.
- What has already been accomplished to fulfill the mission and vision of your organization?
- What has yet to be accomplished to fulfill your mission and vision?
- What are prophetic words concerning your organization's purpose, identity, and destiny?
- What must be done but cannot be accomplished in this season and why?

- What miracles must take place to see the goals of this season fulfilled?

5. *What core values are guiding you in life and leadership?*
When Kathy and I started our auto parts stores, we made choices that determined who we were as a company and how we operated. We had to decide which two of these three core values would define the life of our business:

Price—would we always try to have the cheapest price?
Quality—would we always offer the best parts?
Service—would we provide the best service in the world?

Maybe you are asking, why couldn't you just have the cheapest price, sell the best quality parts, *and* give excellent service all at the same time? Well, it's really simple economics. It costs money to provide great service, because excellent service is directly related to the quality of our people and the number of employees required to service the customers. Quality parts also cost more than the bargain brands. Therefore, if we were going to try to have the lowest price and deliver the highest quality parts while also giving the best service, we wouldn't be able to compete. Our competitors could simply choose to set the best prices, provide great quality parts, and give very little service. Then we would soon go broke trying to fund our great service through the same profit margins as our competitors who were paying thousands of dollars less in payroll.

In the end, we decided that excellent service and

quality parts would be the two core values of our company. We would stay within 5 percent of our competitors' prices and then use the extra money to fund our world-class service.

We were located in a small town of 3,500 people, and we were located an hour from the nearest city, so 90 percent of our business came from the auto-repair shops in town. Our challenge was getting the right parts to our customers as quickly as possible, which meant finding the right warehouses and then delivering products to our customers efficiently.

We did some research and found three huge warehouses that would service us. The closest one was an hour away, and the others were about three hours from us. With an efficient system of communication and an intricate, collaborative delivery scheme, we provided a parts delivery service that made FedEx look like the Pony Express. Our customers could order parts by 10:00 a.m. and receive them by noon. If they ordered parts by noon, they would receive them by 2:00 p.m., and so on. In the evenings, our customers could place orders until 6:00 p.m. and would receive them at 6:00 a.m. the next morning. We made more than $50 million worth of inventory available to our customers, delivered to their doors within two business hours. We maintained our values of quality parts and excellent service, and we eventually found success.

As you can see, nailing down your core values greatly affects the chemistry of your organization and determines who you will be to the world around you. Here are some examples of questions that might help you understand your core values and how they affect your structure:

- Name ten of your personal distinctions, that is, your core values that give you your unique DNA.
- What virtues determine the boundaries of your behavior?
- Which core values dictate what you allow yourself to dream about or desire?
- Which core values do you use to interpret how different events in life relate to God? How do you determine which circumstances in life are attributed to God and which are attributed to the devil?
- Write a motto that will communicate to the people experiencing your organization what to expect from you. For example, our auto parts store motto was, Excellent Service Is the Crossroad Difference.
- What repeated behaviors do you want your core values to inspire in your team?
- What do you want your organization's reputation to be? What do you want to be famous for? What repeated behavior will give you this reputation?

Read this chapter with your team and, as a group, write your answers on a whiteboard. Not only will clarity come from this interaction with your team, but an image or vision of who you are called to be and what you are called to do may emerge.

Now go forward, and structure your holy mission.

12

Chipping Rock

Michelangelo supposedly said, "I saw an angel in the marble, and I carved until I set it free."[1] The difference between chipping rock and freeing angels is the ability to envision imprisoned potential in the stones of life. A monotonous, boring life can be transformed into an exhilarating journey by learning how to capture a vision for your own destiny. Vision gives you the ability to connect the daily grind of life to your eternal purpose. Vision makes life meaningful and gives you the motivation you need to press through the tough seasons.

> THE DIFFERENCE BETWEEN CHIPPING ROCK AND FREEING ANGELS IS THE ABILITY TO ENVISION IMPRISONED POTENTIAL IN THE STONES OF LIFE.

Maybe you are convinced that life will begin when you graduate, get healed, pay off all your bills, get married, or reach any other milestone. But when you make God's promises wait for you to be ready, you undermine your ability to perceive His handiwork in the world around you and miss your divine opportunity to prosper. The truth is that many good people sit on the porch of faithlessness and watch the world go by. Instead, you must anticipate that something meaningful, profound, powerful, and wonderful could happen to you at any moment, because anticipation is the fruit of faith.

Faith inspires vision, that part of us that sees the angel in the marble when everyone else just sees a rock. In fact, everything in the Kingdom is obtained by faith. Faith supersedes your circumstances, overcomes your obstacles, and overrides the facts. Faith sees the invisible, believes the impossible, and empowers the incredible!

The author of Hebrews explained faith in this way: "Now faith is the assurance of things hoped for, the conviction of things not seen. For by it the men of old gained approval. By faith we understand that the worlds were prepared by the word of God, so that what is seen was not made out of things which are visible" (11:1–3).

Faith opens your eyes so you can understand the incomprehensible, and it changes your behavior because you see things that are not yet visible and act on them long before others can. The writer of Hebrews illustrated this beautifully when he wrote this about Moses: "By faith he left Egypt, not fearing the wrath of the king; for he endured, as seeing Him who is unseen" (11:27). Moses saw God, although He is invisible, and therefore Moses left Egypt. In other words, Moses had faith. Faith opened his eyes so he could envision the invisible, which ultimately gave him the courage to defy the most powerful ruler in the world.

Vision

So what exactly is vision, and how do we pursue it? True vision is rooted in His vision, which is inspired by faith, not imagined through selfish ambition. Thus, true vision is foresight with insight that comes from His sight!

Many years ago I became sick of being overweight, so I decided to join a gym to get in shape. I was determined to lose five pounds the first day, so I spent three hours exercising on every machine in the gymnasium. When I woke up the next morning, I was so sore that I had to roll out of bed and crawl to the bathroom. My body hurt in places I didn't even know existed! That was the last time I ever worked out with weights.

I learned something that week: it is very difficult to get skinny by hating being fat, because reacting to a negative rarely creates a positive! Rather, it is vision (in this case, picturing yourself with a healthy body) that causes a person to restrain his or her eating habits, reorder his or her schedule, and push past the discomfort of muscle pain to obtain the goal. Vision gives pain a purpose.

What Do You Think You Are Doing?

In the first *Karate Kid* movie, Mr. Miyagi used practical work (waxing his car, painting his house, and fixing his fence) to teach his protégé, Daniel, karate. But Daniel thought Mr. Miyagi was taking advantage of him by having him do chores around his house. In a rage, Daniel yelled at his mentor, protesting that Mr. Miyagi was using him and not teaching him how to fight.

Mr. Miyagi responded, "Daniel-san, show me how you wax car!" So Daniel demonstrated as Mr. Miyagi corrected his form, repeating, "wax on . . . wax off."

Miyagi then said, "Show me paint the fence." Again, Daniel showed Mr. Miyagi how he painted the fence, while Miyagi adjusted his form, repeating, "up, down, up, down."

Finally, Mr. Miyagi said, "Daniel-san, show me, hammer nail!" And Daniel-san illustrated hammering, while Miyagi again corrected his form. Soon it became clear that Mr. Miyagi had disguised his karate lessons as house projects. Daniel was actually learning how to fight as he waxed the car, painted the fence, and hammered nails. In other words, what you think you are doing is more important than what you are practically accomplishing. Greatness is often hidden in the mundane.

Picture two young men working at a fast-food restaurant grilling burgers. One guy has no vision for his life; he is just watching the clock and flipping burgers. He hates this dead-end job and mourns every minute that he's making kids' meals. The other guy wants to be a great businessman, so he decides to grill burgers the way Solomon's servants waited on tables: with excellence. He challenges himself to grill the best burgers anyone has ever eaten in a fast-food restaurant. He realizes that greatness is often demonstrated when doing ordinary things in an extraordinary way.

Vision is the invisible manager that guides, encourages, and inspires everyday people to change the world. From a distance it may appear that both guys are just flipping burgers, but nothing could be further from the truth. One guy is just working in fast-food, but the other guy has started his business career. Both of them seem to be standing behind the same grill, but the second guy is already sitting behind a huge desk in a plush office, running his multimillion-dollar company.

To be truly successful in life you must envision your future with God; otherwise you don't really know where you are going. When you have no destination, no road can get you there, and running faster won't help you to arrive sooner. Your perception of what you are doing—your vision of the future you are creating—is more significant than what you are actually achieving practically in the moment.

Inspiring Vision

Vision is the pathway to greatness in all walks of life, in every vocation, and in every exploit. You must see it to be it!

"Okay, Kris, I get it, but how do I develop a vision?"

You can't become what you haven't seen or heard. One of the easiest ways to capture a vision is to expose yourself to someone else's dream. For example, let's say you are interested in becoming a ballet dancer. Nothing will awaken your soul like watching someone else who is an extraordinary dancer. Or maybe you want to build a house, but you don't know what kind of home inspires you. Go look at some beautiful houses.

If you are called to be a great leader, read biographies of

famous leaders, interview leaders you admire, and watch personal documentaries. It won't be long before you begin to envision yourself similarly saving the day or accomplishing a great feat. In fact, I encourage you to practice greatness by imagining yourself in the place of someone you are studying.

I have been doing this for twenty years. In fact, I remember reading a biography about George Washington. As the author began to describe the conditions of Washington's troops during the War of Independence, I closed my eyes and imagined myself in his shoes. I began to hear his soldiers moaning as they staggered through the snow-covered woods, their bloody, bare feet staining the path behind them. I felt the conflict within Washington's soul as he was beset with the impossible task of defeating an immense, well-trained British Army with a bunch of ill-equipped, poorly-trained militia farmers. I paced the dirt floor of his ragged tent with him at night as we pondered the suffering of his courageous men who were literally starving to death in the camp.

I joined him as his troops hurried quietly across the Delaware at night to escape the advancing British onslaught. I could feel his heart pounding as he compelled the last of his men into the boats, narrowly eluding capture.

As I journeyed through the pages of the book, I asked myself hard questions: Do I have what it takes to be a courageous leader? Would I have surrendered in light of the immense disparity? How would I have motivated an army of weak, sick men who were out-numbered, fearful, and unfunded? Although I didn't realize it at the time, I was living through George Washington's experiences and envisioning myself as a courageous leader. I imagined being a great leader long before I truly was a good leader.

Working Your Butt Off

Once you have captured that vision, what comes next is a lot of hard work. Vision gives you motivation and energy. It is the cure for apathy and slothfulness. This is not a new idea. In 1921, editors of a local Indiana newspaper encouraged their readers, "The reason most people do not recognize an opportunity when they meet it is because it usually goes around wearing overalls and looking like Hard Work."[2]

The truth is, you were "created in Christ Jesus for good works, which God prepared beforehand" (Ephesians 2:10). You are also commanded by Jesus to work in such a way that people "see your good works, and glorify your Father who is in heaven" (Matthew 5:16). For some reason, though, *work* has become a nasty four-letter word, taught as anti-grace and viewed as the curse of the law. In actuality, hard work is the manifestation of great grace in the life of a believer.

> HARD WORK IS THE MANIFESTATION OF GREAT GRACE IN THE LIFE OF A BELIEVER.

Grace is not only undeserved favor; grace is also the operational power of God. Grace gives you the ability to do what you couldn't do one second before you received grace. Simply put, grace gives you the skill, the motivation, and the unction to work hard.

Many leaders teach that hard work is for those who don't know God, and striving is unspiritual. Actually, the Greek word for striving, *agonizomai,* is used five times in a positive sense in the New Testament alone. Jesus commanded all of us to "strive to enter through the narrow door" (Luke 13:24).

There is a difference between laboring and striving for the Kingdom and laboring and striving with no discernible purpose. Because we live in a performance-driven rat race on an are-we-there-yet? hamster wheel, we often expend huge amounts of time and effort with relatively little to show for it. We can get so busy racing the other rodents that we seldom pause long enough to truly envision our divine destinies.

Vision is the compass that helps us navigate the seasons of life and allows us to dream with God, not just about God. When we dream with God, we cocreate masterpieces of His imagination and ultimately fulfill our divine destinies. In other words, vision gives meaning to our lives and the hard work that successfully extends the borders of the Kingdom. Vision turns hard work into a labor of love, a work of passion.

Courageous Visionaries

Vision is also a catalyst to courage! Of course, being courageous and being fearless are not the same thing. Most people who are fearless live risk-free lives. They are coddled souls who value security over significance and comfort over conquering. People who are courageous, on the other hand, refuse to let their fears dictate their destiny. You might say that "courage is fear that has said its prayers."[3] Courageous people peer into the future and live with a passion to leave a legacy. They confront their fears, take captive their thoughts, and conquer the obstacles that obstruct their divine assignments—those giants inevitably present in every Promised Land.

Andrew Wommack put it this way: "If you never bump into the devil, it's because you are going in the same direction."[4] Often, just about the time you find your divine connection and step into your heavenly purpose, all hell breaks loose. Your inclination might be to retreat to find peace instead of pressing in to obtain your inheritance. It's important for you to understand that the "world forces of this darkness" (Ephesian 6:12) only trouble themselves over world-changers and His-story makers. There is no victory without a

> THERE IS NO VICTORY WITHOUT A BATTLE, NO CONQUEROR WITHOUT SOMEONE CONQUERED, AND NO ARMOR NECESSARY IF THERE IS NO ENEMY.

battle, no conqueror without someone conquered, and no armor necessary if there is no enemy.

It is the process of envisioning your destiny, conquering your fears, and defeating your giants that forges the character you need to live a successful life. Unfortunately, many people reduce their lives to make peace with their fears, thus they never reach their full potential in God. But if you learn how to be courageous in the face of trepidation, you will rise to the heights of your calling and be fully actualized as sons and daughters of God Himself.

13

UNLEASHING HEAVEN

How often have you heard the phrase, "Then all hell broke loose"? What would it look like for you to live in such a way that whenever you encounter tough situations you unleash heaven? I mean, what would happen if you honestly believed you are a son or daughter of the King of the universe, endowed with power and commissioned with authority to disrupt the course of evil and release good wherever you go?

I dream of a day when the people of God are so filled with the Spirit of God that by the Word of God we calm storms, stop earthquakes, and reconcile warring nations. I envision a time not too far into the future when tens of millions of believers unleash heaven wherever they go and thereby shift the atmospheres of nations. In that day, and at that time, it will be commonplace for people to say, "Then all heaven broke loose!"

There are several great examples of this in the Bible. In the Old Testament God commanded Moses to build a gilded, wooden box called the ark of the covenant. On its separate, gilded lid sat two hammered-gold cherubim whose uplifted wings covered the ark and made a throne (sometimes called a "mercy seat") for God's presence. The priests carried the ark on their shoulders with two long, gilded poles wherever the people roamed (Exodus 25:10–22). Wherever that box went, God showed up. In fact, the Israelites took the ark into battle so God would be with them and win the war for them.

When Moses built the tabernacle, he was instructed by God to put the ark of the covenant in the Holy of Holies and to only let the high priest come before the ark once a year.

Centuries later, King David wanted to bring the ark of the covenant into the City of David. He had some guys put the ark on an ox cart to pull it all the way into the city, but the cart hit a bump in the road, and the ark started to fall off the cart. Just then, a guy named Uzzah reached out to steady the ark, and God struck him dead (2 Samuel 6:6–8). David's entire plan ground to a halt, and the ark was taken to Obed-edom's house until David could come up with a better plan. Here's where the story gets really good: The ark was in Obed-edom's barn for three months, and everything that belonged to the guy prospered! In fact, Obed-edom so thrived that rumors of his wealth motivated King David to another way to bring the ark into his city (2 Samuel 6:9–12).

Why did everything at Obed-edom's prosper? Because the presence of God rested on the ark of the covenant. While it was in Obed-edom's possession, the Kingdom was unleashed in his life, and all of heaven broke loose!

You came to Christ through a new covenant, and as it did in the ark of old, the presence of God rests in you. In the same way the cherubim wings protected the ark, you abide under the shadow of the Almighty because He spread His wings over you (see Psalm 91:1–4).

But here is the most intriguing and fascinating part of the story to me: when Obed-edom put the chest in his barn, everybody knew that God was in his house. And when God parks His presence inside of you, He wants everyone to know God is in your house!

"What exactly are you saying, Kris?"

I am saying the force to absolutely positively transform everything in your life (to bless your relationships, fix your finances, heal your body, give peace to your soul, and fully actualize every aspect of your life) is in the presence of God Himself. The Holy Spirit is within you, and His presence can profoundly bless you!

"But, Kris, I don't want to join that self-seeking, narcissistic, egocentric bless-me club!"

Well, probably not, but you should join the Jesus Bless Me Club! What I mean is that when you asked Jesus into your heart, you joined the Bless Me Club, because wherever Jesus lives, He prospers.

Think about how blessed Joseph of the Old Testament was. The guy had a dream that his entire family was going to bow down to him. Unfortunately, he told his family about the dream, because the teenager was kind of arrogant. The next thing he knew, he was a slave in Egypt working for a guy named Potiphar, who was the captain of Pharaoh's bodyguard. But here is the kicker:

The LORD was with Joseph, so he became a successful man. He was in the house of his master, the Egyptian. Now his master saw that the LORD was with him and how the LORD caused all that he did to prosper in his hand. So Joseph found favor in his sight and became his personal servant; and he made him overseer over his house, and all that he owned, he put in his charge (Genesis 39:2–4).

Later when Joseph was falsely accused of raping Potiphar's wife and subsequently thrown in jail,

the LORD was with Joseph and extended kindness to him, and gave him favor in the sight of the chief jailer. The chief jailer committed to Joseph's charge all the prisoners who were in the jail, so that whatever was done there, he was responsible for it. The chief jailer did not supervise anything under Joseph's charge because the LORD was with him; and whatever he did, the LORD made to prosper (Genesis 39:21–23).

Joseph couldn't do anything wrong. He reminds me of those old punching bags we had as kids. They were full of air and were weighted with sand at the bottom. You could hit them as hard as you wanted, but they always popped right back up!

The rest of the story is well-documented and often told. Joseph interpreted a couple of dreams for two prisoners who used to work for Pharaoh, which ultimately led to an audience with the king. Then Joseph interpreted a couple of dreams for Pharaoh and was put in charge of the entire country, becoming as a father to Pharaoh.

Joseph was part of the Bless Me Club. Heaven was unleashed on Egypt because, as He is with you, God was with Joseph and caused everything he did to prosper. (Read the full story in Genesis 37–50.)

Let me remind you of a few others in the Bible who experienced a piece of heaven on earth. There was Samuel the prophet, who grew up in Shiloh's temple. Look what the Bible says about Samuel: "Thus Samuel grew and the LORD was with him and let none of his words fail" (1 Samuel 3:19). Why were Samuel's prophetic words so accurate? Because God didn't let any of Samuel's words go unanswered! How would you like heaven to cosign on every prayer you pray?

Esther is another believer who radiated heaven. She was a Jewish girl in a foreign land who captured the heart of a king. God's favor on Esther's life caused her to be promoted to queen, and she reigned with King Ahasuerus from India to Ethiopia. But, most importantly, the extreme blessing on Esther's life resulted in her people being rescued from annihilation (Esther 1–10).

Let's not forget Moses! Moses went up on a mountain for forty days and talked to God face-to-face. When Moses came down from the mountain, he was literally glowing from being in the presence of God. I mean, the guy was shining so brightly that he had to put a veil over his face to keep the Israelites safe! In fact, every time Moses met with God he lit up like a Christmas tree, and Moses would cover up his face (Exodus 34:29–35). He had an intimate relationship with God, and consequently God showed up and showed off frequently in his life. Saying that heaven was unleashed through Moses is an extreme understatement.

Then there was David, the giant-killing kid, who led sheep

on the back side of the desert. He was a nowhere teenager from a nowhere land born into a nowhere family, but God favored him highly and hand-picked him to be the king of Israel. God Himself proclaimed the ultimate commentary on David's life when Samuel informed King Saul that his successor, David, was "a man after His own heart" (1 Samuel 13:14).

Personally, Daniel is my favorite character in the entire Old Testament. He was a prisoner of war in Babylon. King Nebuchadnezzar, who is arguably the most narcissistic king in the entire Bible, took him captive. This king was so crazy that he made Hitler look like a schoolyard bully, not to mention the fact that he had a desire to be worshiped. If Nebuchadnezzar didn't like you, he just threw your butt in the furnace and watched you burn.

But God granted Daniel favor among the king's officials. Nebuchadnezzar found Daniel to be ten times better than all the magicians, conjurers, and the other wise men of Babylon (Daniel 1). Daniel advised three kings, including King Cyrus who sent the Jews back to Jerusalem to rebuild their city and temple.

You might be asking where I am going with all of this. I want you to understand that God is in you the same way He was on the ark of the covenant! He wants to unleash heaven wherever you go. This list of saints has nothing on you. That wooden box has no advantage over you. You are an open heaven. The presence that changes everything is in you, with you, on you, and through you. You are God's wild card, heaven's X factor, and the incalculable difference maker. The odds might be 100 to 1; but if you are the one and if you know Jesus, then it's foolish to bet against you.

Warning! Warning! Warning!

As you press into God and start seeing the fruit of His presence in your life, it's helpful to know ahead of time that jealousy will be the main side effect of extreme blessing. I love the saying, "If you are successful, you will win false friends and true enemies. Succeed anyway."[1]

A common thread of trouble is woven into everyone who invites the blessing of God into his or her life. Jesus made it clear that if people hated the Savior of the world, they would certainly hate those of us following in His footsteps.

In fact, jealousy enraged the first-century religious leaders in Jerusalem to the point that they actually crucified the God who created them. Jesus drew huge crowds, demonstrated miracles, and stunned the multitudes with His wisdom. But these spiritual leaders (who were once thought of as the holy men of God), when confronted with the reality of relationship which transcended their rules of religion, grew to hate the One who was sent to save their souls.

Not everyone will celebrate your promotions, advancements, or victories. In fact, the more you prosper, the more some people will hate you. Furthermore, they will hate you most for the places of your greatest prosperity. Misery loves company, but misery hates success!

John Dryden received some great advice for us to consider when we are in the middle of this kind of trouble: "It's better to shun the bait than get caught in the snare."[2] Worrying about your detractors is a snare, a massive waste of time. Haters are going to hate! Rather than getting caught up in the judgments of our critics, we can choose to focus on living differently in response to the heaven that has broken loose in our lives.

Jesus said, "From everyone who has been given much, much will be required; and to whom they entrusted much, of him they will ask all the more" (Luke 12:48). I was confronted with this reality a few years ago in a way that rocked me to my core. As you know, Kathy and I had been in business for years and had always been honest in our transactions. But I was taught that it's a dog-eat-dog world out there, and if I didn't look out for number one, nobody else would do it for me. So I took some negotiating classes, read some books, and ultimately learned how to get the best deals, not caring if the other guys made money or not. I reasoned that it was their responsibility to fight for themselves.

But in 2005, I had a powerful encounter with God who, I discovered, wasn't impressed with my self-seeking attitude. He told me in no uncertain terms that my negotiating tactics were instead "manipulation principles based on a lie"!

The conversation went something like this:

God: Kris, do you believe that if you seek first the kingdom of God, then I will take care of everything in your life?
Me: Yes, I think I do.
God: Okay, then it *isn't true* that you have to watch out for yourself because nobody else is. I am looking out for you, and I take better care of you than I do the birds of the air or the lilies of the field. From

now on, you must only negotiate for *win-win*. You
must bless the people you buy from, those who
work for you, and those whom you work with.

God had blessed my endeavors, and I needed to respond to His
blessings by extending the same to others. I had been protecting
myself from the world and hoarding His gifts.

When it came time for us to purchase a new vehicle, Kathy
and I put this into practice. We found the truck we wanted on a
lot at a great dealership in town. Of course, the salesman wanted
us to sit in his office and let the game begin. But we said, "Please
figure out what you think a fair deal is for both of us, and then
call us. We are going to lunch."

He was a little resistant because we refused to play the game,
yet an hour later he called with the dealership's best price. But the
price was too low, so I said, "That's too good of a deal. We want
to pay $1,000 more for the truck." The salesman was so stunned
that he called the owner out of his office and asked us to tell him
about the offer we were making! It was actually quite fun. The
deal was made, and we got a great truck for a fair price. Most
importantly, the Kingdom was demonstrated in a practical way
that day.

The same thing happened last week at a bike shop. We wanted
to buy a couple of new electric bikes, so we went to a place that
one of our friends recommended. The owner turned out to be a
guy who went to our church. He was falling over himself trying
to give us his best price. I finally said, "We didn't come here to get
the best price. We came here to buy great bikes and to bless you

in the process. It would be our privilege to pay full retail for the bikes." The guy was floored!

I hear stories all the time about believers taking advantage of their friendships to get a great deal. We experienced this first-hand when we owned our auto-repair and auto-parts shops. Our "church friends" were often our worst customers. If you want to live a blessed life, then you need to remember that prosperity comes with privileges and responsibilities. When God blesses us, it's incumbent on us to turn around and do the same for others: to help the poor, encourage the fainthearted, strengthen the weak, and give sacrificially. This is the way of God's royal lineage. This is the responsibility of the noble sons and daughters of the King.

Things to Remember

As our journey comes to a close, I want to remind you that when you have Jesus living in you, you have everything you need to rise above the trials of life and become the person you were created to be in God. Refuse to be reduced by your fears, restricted by your past, or derailed by your critics or your worst day. Instead, live as a believer who rises to the high call of God in Christ Jesus and thus becomes fully actualized in your personhood.

> REFUSE TO BE REDUCED BY YOUR FEARS, RESTRICTED BY YOUR PAST, OR DERAILED BY YOUR CRITICS OR YOUR WORST DAY.

Champions are forged in the crucible of life and are molded

by the Potter's hands, which often look familiar, human, and anything but divine. There are times when the hands of the Potter seem to be forcefully working the clay of your life, painfully shaping you into a different vessel for greater glory. Yet at the end of the day, when the wheel has ceased and the noise has stopped, you find peace in the depths of your soul, knowing you yielded your heart to the Master.

Jesus' twelve disciples weren't exactly Fortune 500 CEOs, but something powerful happened to them as they hung out with Jesus. They spent three and a half years on the Potter's wheel and were molded into champions. Even the guy who denied Jesus three times was a force to be reckoned with who became a famous world-changer, the head of the first-century church.

On the other hand, Saul was a self-righteous Pharisee, who himself was responsible for stoning thousands of believers to death. But when Jesus confronted Saul on the road to Damascus, his life changed forever. Saul was molded for about thirteen years on the Potter's wheel before he became the great apostle Paul, who wrote as many as thirteen books of the Bible and spread the gospel all over the world.

Many people make excuses as to why they can't be champions, winners, or world-changers. They think they're not smart enough, spiritual enough, strong enough, or liked enough to be great. But nothing could be further from the truth. God loves to form winners out of chumps, wimps, and weaklings. Paul said it best: "God has chosen the foolish things of the world to shame the wise, and God has chosen the weak things of the world to shame the things which are strong" (1 Corinthians 1:27).

Never underestimate God's ability to take the broken pieces

of your life and remold you into something beautiful. In his book *Developing the Leader Within You*, John Maxwell tells the story of a quality-control consultant who said, "If the process is right, the product is guaranteed."[3] If you submit your life to the "God process," your nobility is guaranteed.

Remember that no matter where you are in life, or how you might be feeling right now, Jesus believes in you. He is bigger than your worst mistake, better than your worst day, and more powerful than your worst circumstances. Put your trust in Him; you will never regret it. After all, you are destined to win!

NOBILITY ASSESSMENT TEST

You often read a book like this with a deep sense of introspection. The manuscript becomes a kind of mirror that you peer into, hoping to catch an honest glimpse of the winning attributes you possess. With this in mind, I devised a short test to help you get a better picture of where you are in your lifelong journey to nobility. I challenge you to approach this test with an open heart. Allow God to affirm you in your strengths and likewise shine His gracious light on the areas of your life that are weak and/or broken. Remember, you can't conquer what you refuse to confront, and you can't confront what you can't see.

Definition of *nobility*:

- Having or showing fine personal qualities or high moral principles and ideals

Attributes of *nobility*:

- virtuousness, goodness, honor, decency, integrity, generosity, selflessness, loyalty, honesty, hard work, courage, love

Directions

You are called to be a noble person, a winner, and a champion. This test is designed to give you an idea of how well you carry yourself as a noble person. For this test to be beneficial, it is necessary for you to be as honest with yourself as you can be. Rank how often you agree with the statements below according to the Scoring Guide. Answer in a way that reflects who and how you are on an average day, not on the best or worst day of your life.

Scoring Guide

0= Never 1= Rarely 2= Sometimes 3= Often 4= Very Often
5= Always

Part 1

1. _____I fear I am not good enough and/or that I don't measure up.
2. _____I often find myself secretly competing with others.
3. _____I compare myself to others often and wish I was someone else.
4. _____I am uncomfortable around wealthy and/or successful people.
5. _____I build cases against powerful people.
6. _____I feel bad about myself when I am not accomplishing something.
7. _____I spend a lot of time wondering what people think about me.
8. _____I tell people what I think they want to hear instead of my real opinion.

9. ____I only feel comfortable around broken or needy people.

10. ____I get jealous when my close friends have other friends.

11. ____I don't set goals, so I don't fail my own expectations.

12. ____I become overly attached to anyone who takes an interest in me.

13. ____I am offended easily.

14. ____I choose less-gifted people to work with me on projects.

15. ____My sex drive and/or eating habits seem to be out of control.

16. ____I often feel that something is about to go wrong.

17. ____I live with a lot of regret for my past mistakes and/or sins.

18. ____I worry a lot about the future.

19. ____I struggle with forgiving others.

20. ____I take it personally and feel rejected when someone disagrees with me.

Add up the points next to each statement, and record the number on the line provided. When you have finished, continue by addressing the statements in Part 2.

_____ TOTAL FOR PART 1

Part 2

21. ____I enjoy investing in people and seeing them outgrow me.

22. _____I like being around free thinkers and creative people.

23. _____I like to create environments where people learn to think.

24. _____I love and enjoy myself.

25. _____I feel comfortable around just about anyone.

26. _____I tend to attract important and successful people around me.

27. _____I choose people to be on my team who have different perspectives.

28. _____I live in peace most of the time.

29. _____I am passionate about what I do.

30. _____I am motivated by the vision I have for my life.

31. _____I am hard to offend.

32. _____I dream about making a dramatic impact on the world.

33. _____I expect people to like me.

34. _____I like to help others discover and obtain their dreams.

35. _____I am a self-starter.

36. _____I am a good listener.

37. _____I control my natural passions for eating, sleeping, and sex.

38. _____I set goals for the areas of my life where I have responsibility.

39. _____I'm aware of my strengths, my gifts, and my weaknesses.

40. _____I take responsibility for my failures and refuse to blame others for them.

Add up the points next to each statement in Part 2, and record the number on the line provided.

_____ TOTAL FOR PART 2

Determining Your Nobility Score

Transfer your points to the lines below. Make sure you enter Part 2 on the first line. Subtract Part 1's points from Part 2's.

_____-_____ = _____

PART 2   MINUS PART 1   FINAL SCORE

NOTE: Your final score can be a negative number.

Plotting Your Nobility Score

On the scale below, mark the position of your nobility score with an X.

Slave -100 -90 -80 -70 -60 -50 -40 -30 -20 -10 **0** +10
+20 +30 +40 +50 +60 +70 +80 +90 +100 Noble

Retake the test in a few months to track the development of your noble attributes.

This test is not the last word on your noble character. It is simply a tool to help you see yourself in contrast to the royal attributes that we have addressed throughout this book. You might find it helpful to let a couple of close friends consider these statements "as you" so you can understand the way other people perceive you. The difference between their test results and yours can reveal a lot about you. It's common to discover that the way you think people perceive you and the way they *actually* perceive you are quite different. Maybe the emperor (you) has no clothes on or maybe he (you) wears royal garments but doesn't know it.

God bless your noble efforts to be a winner in Him!

NOTES

CHAPTER 2: FROM THE INSIDE OUT

1. Marilyn Monroe, *My Story* (New York: Stein and Day, 1974), 47.
2. Harold Eberle, conversation with the author, 2016.
3. Bill Johnson and Kris Vallotton, *The Supernatural Ways of Royalty: Discovering Your Rights and Privileges of Being a Son or Daughter of God* (Shippensburg, PA: Destiny Image, 2006); Kris Vallotton, *Developing a Supernatural Lifestyle: A Practical Guide to a Life of Signs, Wonders, and Miracles* (Shippensburg, PA: Destiny Image, 2007); Kris Vallotton, *Basic Training for the Prophetic Ministry*, expanded ed. (Shippensburg, PA: Destiny Image, 2014); *School of the Prophets: Advanced Training for Prophetic Ministry* (Grand Rapids: Chosen, 2015).

CHAPTER 3: THE WEAK THINGS CONFOUND THE WISE

1. Brené Brown, "The Power of Vulnerability," address, TEDxHouston, June 2010, TED video, 20:19, https://www.ted.com/talks/brene_brown_on_vulnerability.

CHAPTER 4: YOUR DESTINY IS IN YOUR PEOPLE

1. See http://jwa.org/encyclopedia/article/orpah-midrash-and-aggadah and http://www.come-and-hear.com/sotah/sotah_42.html.
2. Jim Collins, *Good to Great: Why Some Companies Make the Leap . . . and Others Don't* (New York: HarperCollins, 2001), 13.

CHAPTER 6: SURROUNDED BY IDIOTS

1. "25 Most Influential Evangelicals in America, Douglas Coe," *Time*, February 7, 2005, http://content.time.com/time/specials/packages /article/0,28804,1993235_1993243_1993262,00.html.
2. George Bush, "Remarks at the Annual Prayer Breakfast," February 1, 1990, in *Public Papers of the Presidents of the United States: George Bush, 1990* (Washington: U.S. Government Printing Office, 1991), 135.
3. Hillary Rodham Clinton, *Living History* (New York: Scribner, 2003), 168.
4. *Hearings on Global Climate Change, Before Senate Environment and Public Works Committee*, 110th Cong. (March 21, 2007) (statement of Al Gore, former Vice President of the United States).
5. Vince Pfaff, quoted in John C. Maxwell, *JumpStart Your Leadership: A 90-Day Improvement Plan* (New York: Center Street, 2014), Hachette e-book, day 71.
6. Doris Kearns Goodwin, *Team of Rivals: The Political Genius of Abraham Lincoln* (New York: Simon and Schuster, 2005).

CHAPTER 9: FORGED IN THE FURNACE

1. *Rocky Balboa*, directed by Sylvester Stallone (2006; Culver City: Sony Pictures Home Entertainment, 2007), DVD.

CHAPTER 12: CHIPPING ROCK

1. Although there is no evidence that Michelangelo spoke these words, the sentiment may have been inspired by his creation of the *Giant* in Florence, Italy, as described in 1553 by his friend and historian Ascanio Condivi in Vita di Michelangelo Bvonarroti (*The Life of Michelagnolo Bvonarroti*), ed. D. B. Updike (1904), 21–23.
2. "Pickups," *Pharos-Tribune* (Logansport, IN), May 18, 1921.
3. Karle Wilson Baker, "Courage," in "Three Small Poems," *Poetry: A Magazine of Verse*, October 1921, 16.
4. "How to Be Happy," *Andrew Wommack Ministries*, June 4, 2007, http://www.awmi.net/reading/teaching-articles/be_happy/.

CHAPTER 13: UNLEASHING HEAVEN

1. Kent M. Keith, "The Silent Revolution: Dynamic Leadership in the Student Council," pamphlet (Cambridge, MA: Harvard Student Agencies, 1968).

2. "To my honoured Kinsman, John Dryden, of Chesterton in the County of Huntington, Esq.," *The Poems of John Dryden* in *The British Poets. Including Translations. In One Hundred Volumes*, vol. 23 (Chiswick: C. Whittingham, College House, 1822), 2:207.

3. John C. Maxwell, *Developing the Leader Within You* (Nashville: Thomas Nelson, 1993), 43.

Follow Kris Vallotton on social media

 Facebook.com/kvministries

Twitter.com/kvministries

Instagram.com/kvministries